T0267183

POLYVAGAL
PROMPTS

POLYVAGAL PROMPTS

FINDING CONNECTION

AND JOY THROUGH

GUIDED EXPLORATION

DEB DANA AND COURTNEY ROLFE

W. W. NORTON & COMPANY

Independent Publishers Since 1923

Note to Readers: Models and/or techniques described in this volume are illustrative or are included for general informational purposes only; neither the publisher nor the author(s) can guarantee the efficacy or appropriateness of any particular recommendation in every circumstance. As of press time, the URLs displayed in this book link or refer to existing sites. The publisher and author are not responsible for any content that appears on third-party websites.

Ladder image From THE POLYVAGAL THEORY IN THERAPY: ENGAGING THE RHYTHM OF REGULATION by Deb Dana. Copyright © 2018 by Deb Dana.

Copyright © 2024 by Deborah A. Dana and Courtney Rolfe

All rights reserved
Printed in China

Frontis © oxygen / Getty Images
Stacked green arches (first on p. viii) © Millaly / iStockPhoto.com
All other art © Mariya Lutskovskaya / iStockPhoto.com

For information about permission to reproduce selections from this book, write to Permissions, W. W. Norton & Company, Inc., 500 Fifth Avenue, New York, NY 10110

For information about special discounts for bulk purchases, please contact W. W. Norton Special Sales at specialsales@wwnorton.com or 800-233-4830

Manufacturing through Asia Pacific
Book design by Lauren Graessle
Production manager: Gwen Cullen

ISBN: 978-1-324-03019-5 (pbk)

W. W. Norton & Company, Inc., 500 Fifth Avenue, New York, NY 10110
www.wwnorton.com

W. W. Norton & Company Ltd., 15 Carlisle Street, London W1D 3BS

1 2 3 4 5 6 7 8 9 0

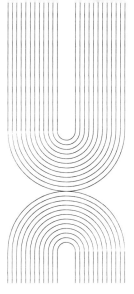

To our fellow autonomic explorers . . .

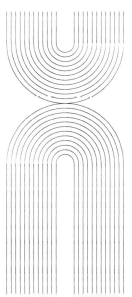

CONTENTS

ACKNOWLEDGMENTS

Writing *Polyvagal Prompts* was an autonomic adventure. Along the way I had moments of joy and moments of wondering how this project would ever come together. It was through the unwavering support and guidance of many others that this book of explorations became a reality. I am reminded each time I begin a writing project that community is an essential element and that connection makes it possible.

First of all, I want to thank Courtney for her passion for bringing Polyvagal Theory to the world and for being a wonderful cocreator. Without her, this project would not have come into being. It was her vision for a guided journal that initiated this project and her tenacity that kept us moving forward. Deep appreciation goes to Deborah Malmud, my editor at Norton, who has been my trusted guide in each of my writing projects. Her commitment to this work, and her wisdom in the ways she shows up to support me, inspires me to keep writing. I'm grateful for my circle of friends who reminded me to trust that I would find the words when I was stuck, and celebrated with me when I did. It is their predictable, welcoming, understanding presence that nourishes my nervous system. And as always, I want to acknowledge Stephen Porges. Steve's brilliant development of Polyvagal Theory is the foundation for my work and makes my writing and teaching possible. His generosity, kindness, and friendship bring joy to my life.

Sending gratitude and a glimmer,
Deb

My greatest gratitude and appreciation go to my mentor, teacher, friend, and coauthor, Deb. Your work has put me on a path of growth and deep exploration. Your support and mentorship have allowed me to bring this work into the world in so many ways. Appreciation also goes to Dr. Stephen Porges, whose research and dedication have given us the information to better understand and connect with our fellow humans. An endless amount of healing has its roots in your work. Thank you to all the people who have included the wisdom of the nervous system in their practices and lives, long before we had a grasp of the technical science behind it.

I am grateful for all the support from within my polyvagal community of co-trainers, colleagues, and learners. I extend great gratitude to the family and friends beyond my polyvagal community. Thank you for checking in on me and for all your encouraging words. I am grateful for each of my clients who have been on this journey with me, and who inspire me every day with their resilience, wisdom, and growth. Thanks to W. W. Norton & Company for all the guidance and support.

And to my wise, kind, loving, fierce, compassionate, encouraging, and regulating partner, Tracy—what a gift it is to have you by my side.

With gratitude,
Courtney

INTRODUCTION

Whether you are a long-time polyvagal enthusiast or a newcomer interested in exploring your nervous system, *Polyvagal Prompts* is an invitation to embark on a guided exploration to discover the remarkable ways your nervous system works in service of your safety and well-being as you navigate the world. Polyvagal Theory, developed by researcher and scientist Dr. Stephen Porges and popularized by social worker Deb Dana, has impacted countless lives. It has changed the way therapists work with their clients and has provided a pathway toward healing for those of us who have experienced hardship or trauma. Looking at life through the lens of the nervous system helps us make sense of our human experience and offers the possibility of living a life rich with curiosity, self-acceptance, compassion, kindness, and a shared sense of humanity. When we understand the biology behind our everyday experiences, we can set aside well-worn narratives about ourselves and others, leave behind stories of self-blame and shame, and step into curiosity about why we think, feel, and act in the ways we do.

Polyvagal Prompts is designed to invite you to explore your nervous system. Using guided prompts, you'll have the opportunity to notice your system, listen with curiosity, and reflect on what you learn. Many of the prompts include an invitation to deepen the practice by taking the concept a step further. If you are well versed in the language of Polyvagal Theory, you will feel right at home and ready to start your journey. If you are new to Polyvagal Theory or want to review the concepts before you begin exploring the prompts, start at the back with the Beginner's Guide to Polyvagal Theory and the glossary of terms.

There are a variety of ways to engage with the prompts. Work with them as a daily practice or explore topics at your own pace. Follow the prompts from cover to cover or hop around and choose the one that fits for you on any given day. No matter how you decide to explore, *Polyvagal Prompts* offers the opportunity to tune into the wisdom of your nervous system, understand the wondrous ways it works, and begin the life-changing journey of befriending your nervous system.

PROMPTS

"When we notice our autonomic experience, we have a chance to engage with it, not simply be engaged by it."

When we notice our state and then name it, we move into awareness of our biology and out of the story our brains create. Naming our experience begins the process of letting go of judgment and self-blame and making room for curiosity. The practice of noticing and naming is fundamental to our polyvagal journey.

Notice what state you are in right now. What are the signs that tell you that's where you are? These could be physical sensations, feelings, thoughts, or behaviors. Use as many clues as you can to help you identify where you are on your autonomic ladder right now.

Taking it a step further: Tracking your movement down and up the ladder gives you a sense of patterns that are happening. If you look back at the past hour, what places have you gone on your ladder? What was your autonomic experience? Extend your reflection. Look back on your day and track your path.

"Autonomic patterns are built over time. The autonomic nervous system is shaped by experience."

While the autonomic nervous system works automatically in the background, we can also take steps to intentionally shape our systems in the direction of regulation. We can learn to move out of survival states and anchor more fully in regulation. When we name our state, take an action, and notice the changes, we are resourcing the pathways that take us out of survival mode and back into safety.

Notice where you are on the ladder at this moment. What can you do to bring a moment of nourishment, care, or kindness to your nervous system? If you are in ventral, how can you deepen this state? Something as simple as a self-hug or allowing yourself a smile may work. If you are in sympathetic, perhaps a breath with a long exhale or connecting with someone you feel safe with could help. If you are in dorsal, notice the shift that can happen in just making a small movement or bringing awareness to your breath. Experiment with small acts to find what helps you take a step toward regulation.

Taking it a step further: Building your own, personalized resource list is an important part of befriending the nervous system. As you experiment over time, you learn what works in each state. Create a list for each state, identifying the small things you can do to nourish your nervous system.

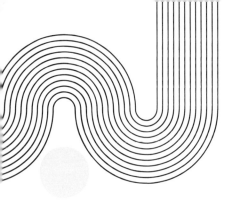

"Ventral vagal energy supports self-compassion—the act of reaching in to be with our own suffering with kindness. In a ventral state, hope arises, and change is possible."

Each of our states impacts our feelings, behaviors, and beliefs in particular ways. It is only from a state of regulation that we can be compassionate, connected, and curious. When we move out of regulation into adaptive survival states, we lose our ability for compassion, connection, and curiosity toward both ourselves and others.

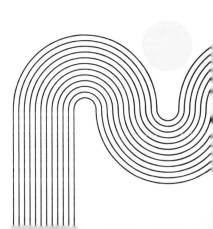

Imagine you have dials for compassion, for connection, and for curiosity. Turning the dial allows more ventral energy into your system and more access to these qualities. Think of a dysregulating situation that you would like to revisit. Decide which quality—compassion, connection, or curiosity—you'd like to explore first. Choose the dial, turn it up, and notice what happens. How does the experience shift and the story change? Now see what happens when you turn up the other two dials. Which is the easiest dial for you to turn and feel an increase of that quality? Which is the hardest? Reflect on how each changes the situation.

Taking it a step further: A dial can be held in your imagination, created on paper, described in words, and brought to life with a movement. Experiment with each way and see what emerges. Find the ways that bring your dials to life.

"The reassuring, heartwarming news is that autonomic flexibility can be shaped over time."

An autonomic intention is a way to bring awareness to our patterns of connection and protection and begin to reshape the ways we respond in our daily lives. We can look at how our nervous system brings ventral connection, sympathetic fight and flight, and dorsal disconnection and set intentions to acknowledge, honor, and work with our patterns. Creating an autonomic intention focuses on reshaping habitual moves into sympathetic or dorsal and deepening the experience of ventral.

Choose a pattern you'd like to change. Write an autonomic intention for the day. Read it out loud and see if your mind and body are in agreement. The intention needs to be strong enough to bring a change but not so big that it's unreachable. Rewrite it in any way you need until you find the words that will help you be successful and feel encouraged to keep going. At the end of the day, reflect on your experience. What worked? What was challenging? Practice writing autonomic intentions and become skillful at bringing your brain and nervous system together in the process.

Taking it a step further: Writing an autonomic intention and holding it over a period of time is a way to work to reshape a particular pattern. Set an intention and stick with it for a week. At the end of the week, notice what has changed. As you reflect on the week, is this an intention you want to continue to work with? Have you met your goal and are ready to move on? Is this a lifelong intention?

> **"Being able to correctly identify autonomic states is the necessary first step in the process of shaping our system in a new way."**

When we know where we are, we know what to do. The first step is to find ourselves on the ladder. The next is to reach for a resource that either deepens our experience of ventral or helps us begin to move out of survival states. From dorsal we need a gentle return of energy, from sympathetic we need to organize the flood of energy, and in ventral we want to celebrate the moment.

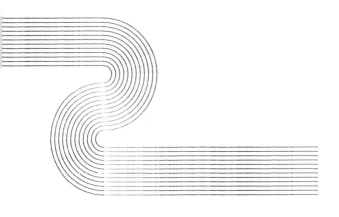

What is your autonomic state at this moment? If you're in ventral, take a moment to tune into your embodied sense of this place of regulation. Are there words that describe this? Or an image or movement that helps you tune in? If you notice you're in sympathetic or dorsal, you've already started the trip up the ladder by naming the state. Just the act of noticing brings a bit of ventral on board! What can you do next to continue to find your way to regulation?

Taking it a step further: Make a list of the resources you discover so you can reach for them when you find yourself in these places in the future.

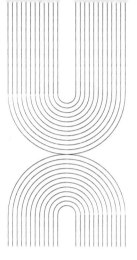

"Glimmers are the micro-moments of ventral vagal experience that routinely appear in everyday life yet frequently go unnoticed."

Humans are built with a negativity bias to help ensure our survival. We're wired to respond more intensely to negative experiences than to equally intense positive ones. If we don't actively look for the micromoments of safety and connection that are our glimmers, they can pass by without our knowing.

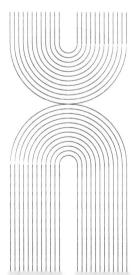

Reflect on your day and see if you can find a glimmer that was on your path, but that you missed at the time. Revisit the moment and feel your ventral energy come alive. Relive it as you remember.

Taking it a step further: Use art to illustrate a glimmer you experienced and want to remember.

"Music is all around us, affecting our physiology and our feelings."

Music accompanies us as we move through our day. It is a powerful activator and regulator of our autonomic nervous system. Music is a doorway to safely connect with, and enjoy, the experience of all three states. When we listen to music, we deepen our connection to ventral and embrace experiences of sympathetic fight and flight and dorsal despair. We listen to a song and feel met, seen, understood, and not alone.

What music most resonates with your sympathetic state? Dorsal? Ventral?
Spend some time listening and noticing. You may be drawn to music with
lyrics, instrumental pieces, certain genres and composers, or you may find
you like a range of musical experiences. Once you've begun to discover what
music moves you, make a polyvagal playlist. Choose three to five musical
selections that bring each of your states alive. Shuffle and play these, and let
the music take you on an autonomic journey.

Taking it a step further: Listening together builds connection. Is there
someone you can share your playlist with?

"Music is a gentle way to travel the hierarchy."

Music moves us. It affects our physiology and our feelings.

Music has paradoxical effects, allowing us to safely connect to,

and even enjoy, our sympathetic and dorsal vagal states

when we listen to certain songs.

Use music to connect to your states with intention and safety. Create a playlist that focuses on the ventral state and build a collection of songs that celebrates the many flavors of ventral, from excited, playful, joyful, passionate, purposeful, to calm, restful, and restorative. Use this playlist to deepen your connection to regulation. Create a playlist for sympathetic and one for dorsal. These playlists bring to life the paradoxical effect music offers of being with suffering in a way that allows you to safely connect with those moments. Reach for these playlists when you feel the pull of sympathetic or dorsal energy and find the way to be with experiences that in the past have been overwhelming, and safely touch those places.

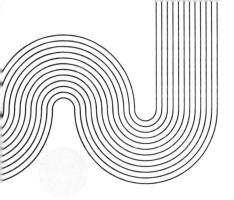

"Our brains say, 'we should' or
'of course' to make a quick decision,
while our nervous systems use 'maybe'
and 'what if' to invite a moment
of contemplation."

The nervous system is always communicating, but we often don't know

how to listen. Learning to listen is a skill, and as we practice tuning in,

we get better at hearing what the nervous system wants us to know.

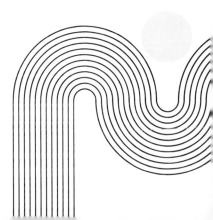

Do you find yourself honoring your nervous system throughout the day, or do you power through the signals that your system is sending? Maybe you remain in a conversation with someone even though your system is telling you that something's not right, or move from one activity to another back-to-back, even though the message you are getting is that you need more time to transition. Remember a time when your nervous system was communicating, and you listened. Now think back to a time when you didn't listen. Reflect on several moments of listening and not listening.

Taking it a step further: Use what you've learned in your listening practice and create a plan to become a better autonomic listener. Identify three simple steps that remind you to tune in and take in the information.

"How we move through the world—turning toward, backing away, sometimes connecting and other times isolating—is guided by the autonomic nervous system."

The autonomic nervous system has an important role in our experiences of approaching, avoiding, and feeling ambivalent. Each autonomic state plays a part in how we say *yes*, *no*, and *maybe*. Knowing the many ways these experiences emerge and being able to identify which state is sending the message are essential skills.

Play with the words *yes*, *no*, and *maybe*. Write each word as it would appear from your sympathetic, dorsal, and ventral states. Use different fonts and colors to capture the essence.

Read your words and notice what happens. What does *no* feel like from sympathetic fight or flight? From the collapse of dorsal? And from the ventral state of regulation? Move to *maybe*. End with exploring the different feelings of *yes*.

When we speak words, they can feel different than when we read them. Experiment with saying *yes*, *no*, and *maybe* from each state. Notice how your experience changes.

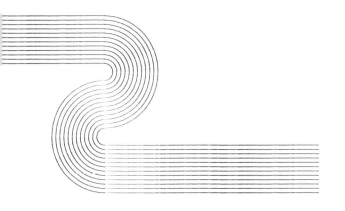

"We live a story that originates in our autonomic nervous system, is sent through autonomic pathways from the body to the brain, and is then translated by the brain into the beliefs that guide our daily living."

Context comes from the Latin word *contexere*, meaning to weave together. Through the lens of the nervous system, context is one of the essential elements of safety. We gather information about how, what, and why to understand, and respond to, experiences.

Think of a recent situation where the lack of context contributed to a survival response. What information would have helped you in that situation? Think of a recent situation where you had enough context to stay regulated. What information was offered that supported your regulation?

Taking it a step further: Create an intention to provide more context to others as you navigate your day. Notice how people respond when you intentionally offer more information.

"Change involves leaning into a pattern that is nourishing and moving away from a pattern that is draining."

Technology is woven into the ways we communicate, learn, work, shop, and play. It is inevitable, unavoidable, and invaluable. Technology can be a resource that brings a sense of safety and connection, and it can also take us into a survival response. We use technology both to feel that we are a part of life and to escape from life.

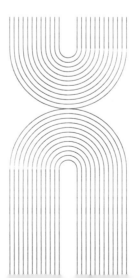

Consider the effect technology has on your autonomic nervous system.
When is it a helpful resource? Perhaps there is music or a podcast you listen
to that promotes a feeling of safety and connection. Maybe your computer
and headphones allow you to connect with a loved one who is far away, or
email helps you stay in touch with friends. When are the times that technology brings distraction and disconnection? Do you get interrupted by messages and calendar reminders throughout the day, disrupting your focus or
your connection to others? Do you find yourself numbing out from the world
by disappearing into a video game or endless episodes of a show? Reflect on
your day and the ways technology influenced your autonomic states.

Taking it a step further: Make a list of the ways technology supports you,
and a list of the ways technology creates barriers to regulation and connection. Identify what you can do to minimize or eliminate technology that is dis-
ruptive and disconnecting and what you can do to deepen your connection
to technology that is regulating and connecting. Experiment with these ideas
for several days. What happened as you leaned into the ways technology is a
resource for you and moved away from the ways it is dysregulating?

"When autonomic patterns begin to change, we find ourselves in the unfamiliar experience of being between—not held in old patterns and not yet predictably in new ones."

Our autonomic patterns change when we repeat small actions over and over. These small changes accumulate and reach a tipping point, leading to a larger change. While the small changes are essential to creating new patterns, they often remain unnoticed, working in the background until we bring awareness to them. Attending to the small changes helps us notice that our system is reorganizing and reminds us that we are on our way to a new pattern of connection.

Think back on your day. Was there an experience that you handled differently than you have in the past? Note what was different about your autonomic response. Was your response less intense or not as long-lasting? Did you stay regulated instead of being pulled into protection or find your way back to regulation more easily than in the past? Look for the small ways your responses are changing.

Taking it a step further: Choose a pattern you want to change and identify a few small actions you can experiment with to begin to move out of that pattern toward a new one. Track the differences in your daily experience for a week. Notice what actions were helpful in making a change and where you got stuck. Continue with the actions that were helpful, look for an action to get unstuck, and experiment for another week.

"**We regularly travel the hierarchy as we navigate the challenges of daily living.**"

The ability to move flexibly between states brings a sense of well-being. We move out of connection into moments of protection and find our way back to regulation many times a day. Classical music has the potential to feed our ventral energy, excite our sympathetic nervous system, and draw us down to dorsal, taking us on an autonomic journey.

What is your experience with classical music? Are you drawn to it? Are there some composers or types of songs that are more welcoming to you than others? Reflect on your relationship with classical music. Go online and find a classical song to listen to. If you're not sure where to start, Smetana's symphonic poem "The Moldau" and Barber's "Adagio for Strings" are wonderful examples of classical songs that have the capacity to take you on an autonomic journey. Play the song you've selected and begin the journey. Pay attention to your nervous system. Where does the music take you? When do you feel the first charge of sympathetic activation coming on board? When do you feel drawn to dorsal? What types of sounds invite ventral into your system? Listen to a variety of classical songs and discover how your nervous system responds to different sounds, rhythms, and melodies.

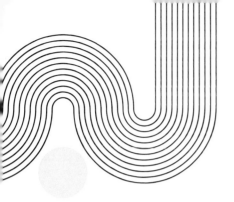

"With 18 breaths per minute, an adult takes 25,902 breaths a day . . . and in each of those breaths, there is an opportunity to shape the nervous system toward safety and connection."

Breath is controlled by the autonomic nervous system. It's an automatic process, but one we can also intentionally manipulate. Breath is a direct pathway to our autonomic nervous system, making it both a regulating resource and an activator of our survival states.

Find your breath. Place a hand on your chest, abdomen, side ribs, small of your back, or under your nostrils, and tune into your breath rhythms. Spend a few moments following your inhalation and exhalation. What do you notice about your natural breath rhythms? Changing the rhythms and cycles of breathing can quickly begin to shift our autonomic state. Take a few moments to play with breath and notice how your state changes. First, try a few breaths with a long inhale and a short burst of an exhale. Did that pull you closer to ventral or activate a survival state? Try a few breaths with a natural inhale and a long, extended exhale. Where does that take you? Experiment with a variety of ways of breathing. Listen to the stories that accompany your breath.

"Glimmers offer a reminder that our nervous systems can hold both dysregulation and regulation—that our days can be filled with difficulty, and we can also feel a spark of ventral safety."

When we feel a spark of ventral energy, we experience a glimmer. Glimmers are all around us, but from a state of protection they are hard to find, and even when we are anchored in ventral, we can miss them if we're not looking. When we actively notice, name, and keep track of glimmers, they add up, and we build a foundation of regulation.

Reflect on your day and notice the glimmers you encountered. Make a list of your glimmers and then spend a few moments savoring your list. The more you practice identifying and naming glimmers, the more you create a habit of inviting them into your awareness in everyday experience.

Taking it a step further: Keep a glimmer journal for a week and reflect on what is different after the week of tracking your glimmers. Notice any shifts in your states and how your view of the world may have changed. Consider whether this is a practice you want to incorporate into your daily life.

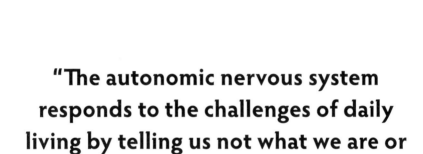

"The autonomic nervous system
responds to the challenges of daily
living by telling us not what we are or
who we are but how we are."

We are touched by a moment. Our autonomic nervous system tells us
when something feels significant. Learning to pause and listen is part
of the process of befriending our nervous system.

What was an experience that really touched you today? Take a moment and revisit that experience. How did you feel? When you reflect on this experience, where in your body do you notice the feeling to be strongest? In your heart region, in your gut, in your face, head, or eyes, in your throat, or somewhere else? Place a hand on that spot and notice what happens.

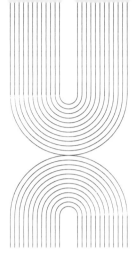

"Through understanding how the autonomic nervous system takes in embodied, environmental, and relational experiences, we become active operators of our systems and authors of our own autonomic stories."

Our nervous system is constantly tracking cues of safety and danger in every environment we enter. Through neuroception, we pick up on these cues and use them to assess our safety in a space. Environments have many elements that communicate safety and danger. Sounds, temperature, colors, textures, space, light, and design all impact our autonomic experience.

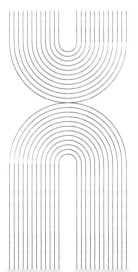

Reflect on the places you visited today. Notice how your state shifted as you moved from place to place. How did the spaces you visited affect your overall autonomic experience today?

Taking it a step further: When you become aware of how a space influences your state, you can begin to shape your environment in ways that invite ventral regulation. Reflect on the places you regularly move through that feel welcoming and enliven your ventral state. Notice specifically what it is about these spaces that brings a sense of comfort. Now reflect on a place that challenges your sense of connection and consider one change you could make to add an element of safety. Make the change and see what happens.

"Haiku captures a moment in time in just a few words."

Haiku is a form of Japanese poetry made up of three lines and seventeen syllables. The first line has five syllables, the second has seven syllables, and the third, again, has five syllables. Writing a haiku invites us to identify the essence of an autonomic moment. The only rules for writing a haiku are the number of lines and syllables. This is an invitation to play with words and see what emerges.

Write a haiku that expresses your experience of a moment in each state— dorsal, sympathetic, and ventral. As you read your poems, notice how your energy follows the state you are expressing.

Here are some examples:

Dorsal:
How long have I sat
No voice, no movement, slow breath
Far away from you

Sympathetic:
Look around, danger
Who is safe and who is not?
Get me out of here

Ventral:
A bright heart beaming
Wrapping all with love and warmth
Holding space for you

Taking it a step further: Create a series of poems by writing a haiku each day for a week. Reflect on the autonomic journey expressed in your poems. Notice the ways your nervous system takes you there again as you read and remember.

"Autonomic state shifts in response to the challenges of daily life are a normal and expected experience. The goal is to not always be in a state of ventral regulation but rather to be able to flexibly navigate the small ordinary shifts that are a part of everyday life."

Everyday living is a complex experience of navigating our way through states. We move in and out of ventral regulation naturally over the course of the day. By noticing our autonomic experience, we develop the ability to name our states and recognize when we move from state to state.

Use the following prompts to reflect on the autonomic path you traveled today. What state did you wake up in this morning? How did your state shift as you began moving through your day? Where was your nervous system by the time you reached midday? How did your state shift as you moved through the afternoon, then evening? Where are you on your ladder right now? Describe the ups and downs of your day through the lens of the autonomic nervous system.

Taking it a step further: Use this information to illustrate the journey your autonomic nervous system took you on today.

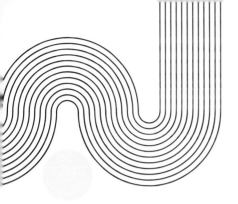

"Glimmers gently yet significantly shape our systems toward well-being. Once we learn to look for glimmers, we find they are all around us and we begin to look for more."

Glimmers are not limited to out-of-the-ordinary experiences. They can be found in predictable places, including our everyday spaces and daily routines. Sometimes glimmers become such a regular part of our daily activities that we forget that they are in fact glimmers.

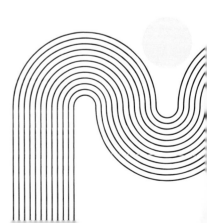

What are some glimmers that showed up today in your everyday routine?
Perhaps you had a moment to snuggle a pet. Maybe your coffee was exactly the right temperature this morning or you noticed a new leaf emerging from a plant in your home or yard. List as many glimmers as you can find from your day today.

Taking it a step further: Write about what a typical day looks like for you. Then, look for a glimmer that is reliably available to you during each part of your day.

"What our nervous system knows and will do to help us survive is quite amazing . . . and undeniable."

The autonomic nervous system doesn't attach moral meaning to states and state changes. It simply acts in service of our survival. While the actions may not bring the desired result, or may feel irrational or even unhealthy, the autonomic intention is always to keep us safe. Recognizing the protective intent from a place of nonjudgment is part of the process of befriending the nervous system.

Reflect on your day and notice the ways your nervous system acted to protect you. Write a note of appreciation to one of the autonomic states that acted in service of your safety.

Taking it a step further: Read the note you've written to your survival state. Take time to listen for a response from your nervous system. What do you hear or feel?

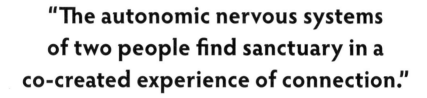

"The autonomic nervous systems of two people find sanctuary in a co-created experience of connection."

Biologically, we know we need connection to safe people in our lives to cultivate a sense of well-being. We are truly wired to connect. Just as we receive cues of safety from others, we also pick up on cues of danger that move us out of connection into survival states.

Reflect on the people you connected with during your day today. These can be people you were in contact with or people you simply thought about. Notice who brought you a sense of ventral connection, who activated your sympathetic nervous system, and with whom you felt a pull into dorsal. Did you come across anyone with whom you shared a sense of playfulness? Was there someone you felt comfortable with sharing a moment of quiet?

Taking it a step further: Reflect on the interactions that pulled you away from ventral and visualize being in that experience offering ventral regulation again. What does the situation feel like when you bring more ventral into the picture? How does it change your sense of your relationship with this person?

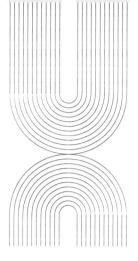

"With the many moving pieces of people and connections that make up our lives, there is often a chaotic mix of autonomic energies. The goal is to navigate with flexibility."

Reshaping our nervous systems toward connection and regulation is an ongoing and intentional process. Every day we can discover what activities or actions bring safety and regulation to our system.

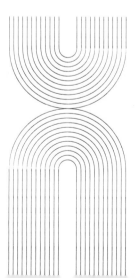

What resources did you use to stay in a more connected place today?
What were some things you did today that helped you find your way back from a moment of dysregulation?

Taking it a step further: Write an intention to continue to use one or more of the resources you identified. What are some ways you might create more reliable access to them? For example, if you felt more anchored in ventral after texting with a friend, perhaps you can set an intention to contact at least one person you feel connected to at some point each day. If you were able to squeeze in a brief, nourishing walk today, perhaps you can find a way to incorporate that in the rest of the days in your week.

"The autonomic nervous system is a common denominator in our human family."

As we navigate the world, we unconsciously broadcast either a welcome or a warning to the people around us. These messages are communicated through our tone of voice (prosody), facial expressions, eye gaze, words, and body language. Because we are wired to co-regulate, the message we broadcast can have a powerful impact on other nervous systems.

Think of a time today when you may have influenced another autonomic nervous system. How did you use your eyes, voice, words, and body language to send a welcome or warning?

Taking it a step further: Think of your ventral energy as a resource that can be offered to everyone around you. Navigate your day with the intention of broadcasting a ventral welcome. At the end of the day, reflect on what the experience was like for you. Be curious about anything that felt different.

"We can be surprised by the creativity of our internal world to bring our autonomic experiences to life."

The way we represent the qualities of our autonomic nervous system states is only limited by our imagination. When we explore in different ways, we deepen our understanding of our states of safety and survival.

If you could choose an animal to represent each of your nervous system states, what animals would you choose and why? What are the qualities that drew you to each? Find an illustration or a video of each animal that captures the essence of the state for you. Notice how the images or videos align with your states.

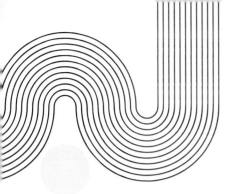

"The autonomic nervous system is at the heart of our lived experience."

Each day is a new opportunity to learn more about our nervous system and how it works to protect us. By repeating the notice-and-name practice multiple times and in many ways, we move into a deeper understanding.

Reflect on your autonomic journey today and play with a new way of expressing it. You might write a story, poem, or song, create a dance or a series of movements, or draw a picture.

"Beneath the level of conscious awareness our nervous system directs our movement toward and away from people, places, and experiences."

Before the brain can put feelings and thoughts into language,

the nervous system initiates a response that moves us toward

an experience and into connection, takes us into the mobilizing

protection of fight and flight, or rescues us through shutdown and

disconnection. When we tune into our nervous system, we bring

awareness to this otherwise nonconscious experience.

What is your nervous system state at this moment? If you're in ventral, take a moment to tune in to your embodied sense of regulation and connection. If you're in sympathetic or dorsal, what is a regulating resource you can bring in to help you move up the ladder?

Taking it a step further: Create a list of things you could do to move up the ladder when you are pulled into sympathetic or dorsal protection. Make one list for each survival state. Then make a list of ways you can strengthen your ventral experience when you are anchored in regulation. Reach for your list when you find yourself in a survival state or want to deepen your sense of regulation. Remember, you've already created the list—now you just need to choose something to try.

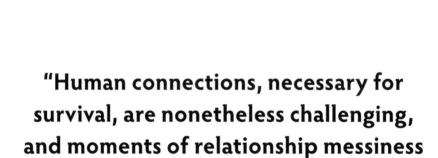

"Human connections, necessary for survival, are nonetheless challenging, and moments of relationship messiness are common."

Some people in our lives bring our ventral state of safety and connection alive, while others present a challenge to our nervous system, triggering the survival energy of sympathetic or the collapse of dorsal. Over time, through repeated experiences, our autonomic responses become habitual patterns.

Reflect on the people you encountered today. What states were activated with each person? Track this over time—a few days or even a few weeks. Reflect on any patterns you notice with the people you regularly encounter in the world. Which relationships are a consistent source of ventral safety for you? Which relationships tend to activate a survival response?

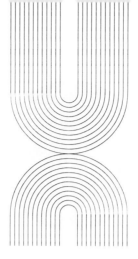

"There is no right or wrong way. There is just the way of your nervous system."

One of the essential elements that our nervous systems need to feel safe is choice. Some days we are drawn toward one experience, and other times we choose a different path. Having options and making a mindful choice deepens our ability to anchor in ventral.

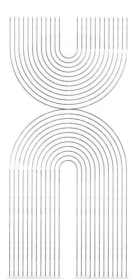

Review the following four reflection prompts and choose the one that you are drawn to at this moment.

Write about one of the following:

  Your current nervous system state
  A glimmer you experienced today
  A ventral vagal connection you had today
  Your autonomic journey today

"We are social beings who also need times of solitude."

While we are all wired for connection, we have different levels of need for solitude and social engagement. Solitude is an experience that nourishes our nervous system. And yet there is a point for each of us when too much solitude turns into an experience of loneliness. Unlike solitude, loneliness is characterized by suffering and negatively affects our sense of physical and emotional well-being.

Reflect on the difference between solitude and loneliness. How can you tell which is a ventral state and which is sympathetic distress or dorsal disappearing? Make a list of the indicators that help you identify your state. Perhaps reading a book is a safe, solitary ventral experience, sending a stream of texts is a sympathetically fueled action, and getting absorbed in playing games on your phone is an experience of dorsal disappearing.

Taking it a step further: Track your experience over the course of the week. Notice the patterns. When do you most often find yourself in comfortable solitude? When do you most need this? What are the times you get pulled into sympathetic or tend to disappear into dorsal? What do you notice is happening that day, that hour, or just before a survival state takes over?

"Through co-regulation we connect with others and create a shared sense of safety."

Our nervous systems find safety and stability in connection with others. When I feel safe with you and you feel safe with me, we move toward connection and into co-regulation. We all carry the ongoing need to connect with others, and every day we long for and look for opportunities to co-regulate.

Reflect on your relationships with an eye for matches and mismatches.
Your nervous system is sometimes a great match for another nervous system, bringing a sense of ease and comfort. Other times you find there's a mismatch, and you feel unsettled or even a bit unsafe. What are the signs that tell you whether it's a match or a mismatch? Use this awareness to look at the people in your life and notice who is a great autonomic match and who is a mismatch.

Taking it a step further: What would happen if you let this sense of match and mismatch guide your future interactions with people? Is there room to more often say no to somebody who is not a ventral resource for you? Are there ways to further invite in the connections that do bring you safety and nourishment?

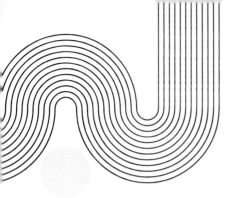

"I love the smell of the sea and pine trees. These are the smells of home for me. I light a scented candle and find my way to regulation."

Scents impact the way we experience the world. They evoke an autonomic response. Fragrance is all around us, activating survival energy or inducing a sense of calm. Some scents seem to have a universal effect, but many are experienced personally.

Think about your experience with smell. What scents elicit calm, ease, excitement, intrigue, or even danger? What scents affect you the most? Notice which bring a survival response and which bring your ventral energy alive. Are there some you would reach for to help you navigate back to regulation?

Taking it a step further: Create a collection of scents you can use as resources. Perhaps something strong like eucalyptus or peppermint pulls you from dorsal, something calming like lavender or vanilla helps you move out of sympathetic, and something grounding like citrus or rosemary deepens your sense of being anchored in ventral. Create a list of the scents that are most effective for you. Play with different scents through foods, candles, essential oils, incense, or other ways that help you build a scent collection that nourishes your autonomic nervous system. Find the fragrances your autonomic nervous system finds renewing.

"Glimmers are a reminder that ventral energy is always around waiting to be noticed and nourish our nervous systems."

Glimmers from one day make us curious about what we'll find the next day. Once we begin to see glimmers, we look for more and discover they are not uncommon experiences. When we are open to finding them, glimmers show up frequently in our daily lives.

Some glimmers are reliably available, and others are found in unexpected places. Reflect on the predictable places and times glimmers routinely appear for you. Notice a recent glimmer that took you by surprise.

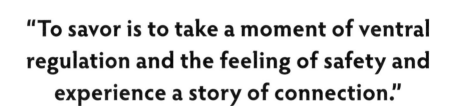

"To savor is to take a moment of ventral regulation and the feeling of safety and experience a story of connection."

Savoring brings to life a ventral moment to intentionally appreciate the experience. It is a practice of capturing and deepening a ventral moment. When we savor, we focus on the thoughts, feelings, and sensations brought to life in a ventral vagal moment.

Look for a ventral vagal moment that happened today that you'd like to savor. Spend 10 to 20 seconds remembering and reliving the experience. Notice how your system experiences this ventral moment.

Taking it a step further: Write a savoring intention to create a practice of stopping to take in a ventral moment.

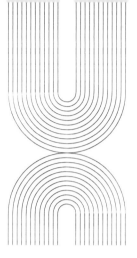

"Glimmers build the foundation for our well-being."

Bringing intentionality and awareness to the presence of glimmers in our day is a practice that helps us more easily recognize the ventral resources that exist in our everyday lives.

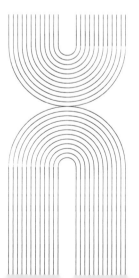

Jot down as many glimmers as you can think of as you reflect on your day.
Try to fill up the entire space on this page! You may have to dig deep, but
when you take the time to look for them, you often find tiny moments of
abundance in your day-to-day life. If this exercise feels like a healthy stretch,
then you are helping your system grow and expand in its capacity. If at any
point this exercise feels like it crosses the threshold from stretch to stress,
it's important to honor your nervous system and pause. Stretching is how
you grow, but stressing elicits a survival response. This exercise may be an
opportunity to tune in to the subtle difference between the two.

"Autonomic regulation and a story of safety happen when the heart and the breath are in harmony."

Neuroception pays attention to what is going on inside our bodies to assess safety and danger by listening to heart and breath rhythms, digestion, aches and pains, and places of relaxation.

Take a moment and listen inside. What is an internal cue of danger your neuroception is detecting? You might feel pain or tension in your body, a sense of unease in your gut, or a sense of restlessness. What is an internal cue of safety? Maybe you notice your breath is steady and slow, you feel warm and relaxed, or supported by your feet on the ground. Explore all the ways neuroception is sending you cues of safety and danger through this embodied pathway.

Taking it a step further: Make a list of ways your body regularly sends you cues of safety and danger. Use your list to tune in and track where your neuroception is taking you.

"We can think about our moment-to-moment experience as an equation. Because the nervous system is always taking in cues, the safety/danger equation is always changing."

We can understand our experiences of safety and danger through a simple equation. When the signs of safety outnumber or outweigh the signs of danger, we are ready to engage with life, and when the signs of danger outnumber or outweigh the signs of safety, we move into a survival response. To tip the balance toward safety, we need to reduce or resolve signs of danger and connect with signs of safety.

Imagine your signs of safety and danger in the form of two simple lists.
Reflect on an experience and create two lists—one for the signs of danger you notice and one for the signs of safety. First look at the number of signs and then identify the most potent signs on both lists. Reflect on whether you feel invited into safety or pulled into survival.

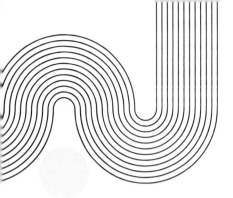

"It is not enough to resolve cues of danger. We must also experience cues of safety."

When a survival state is activated, we naturally pay attention to the cues of danger and because of that, miss the cues of safety that may also be present. When we bring awareness to the cues of danger and become curious about cues of safety, it's possible to see an experience differently.

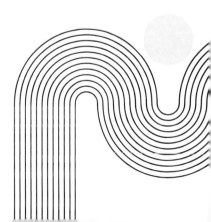

Reflect on a moment during the day when a survival state was activated.
Notice the cues of danger your neuroception picked up on. Then look for
any cues of safety that you might have missed. How does this change your
sense of the experience? Take a moment and write the story of that moment
with this new information.

"We come into the world wired to connect."

Through our biology we are wired for connection. Many of us live in a culture that encourages independence, but we need to remember we are meant to live in connection. Connection is an essential element in feeling safe and regulated.

Look back on your day and see if there was an experience of connection that brought you into ventral regulation. Reflect on this experience. Now see if there was an experience where there was a lack of connection. How did you respond? Were you able to stay anchored in ventral and be curious, or did you feel the stirring of a survival state?

"Choice is an essential element for a regulated nervous system."

Having the right amount of choice in any given moment is essential to
feeling safe and regulated. No choice, not enough choice, or unlimited
choice can take us into a survival state.

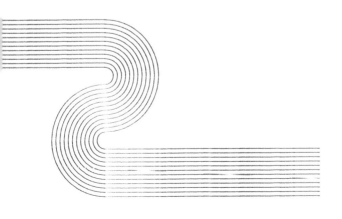

Reflect on the role of choice in how you experienced your day. Was there a situation where the lack of choice or too much choice brought a survival response? Can you think of a situation where the amount of choice contributed to feeling safe?

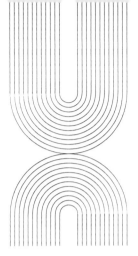

"With regular practice, our nervous system's capacity for flexibility is resourced."

Predictability often brings a sense of safety. Rituals are symbolic actions we follow in set, purposeful ways. Simple rituals are a powerful way to enliven ventral energy and calm our survival systems.

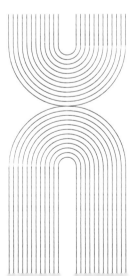

Reflect on the rituals you regularly engage in that bring ventral energy to your system. Take a moment to write about them.

Taking it a step further: Would you like to create a new ritual? Write your intention. Design the flow of your ritual. Identify any objects you want to include or external resources that you need to bring your intention to life.

"Experiences in nature also bring the ventral state alive."

Nature reliably enlivens our ventral state, and when we are cut off from the natural world, we feel the disruption. The sights and sounds of nature are regulating and restorative.

Explore different environments and see what calls to you. Where are the places that feed your soul? Head outside and take a walk. Notice any ways your nervous system shifts from the start to the end of your walk. What feels different?

"Nature, both in real life and through viewing images, offers relaxing and restorative opportunities."

We have a ventral response, not only to being out in nature but to viewing images of nature. While we are not always able to directly access nature, watching videos or looking at pictures of nature also brings us to the place of ventral regulation.

Find images or videos of nature that bring your ventral state alive.
Reflect on your autonomic experience when you spend time with each image or video. Notice what flavor of ventral energy comes alive with each. Create a practice of engaging with your images or videos regularly.

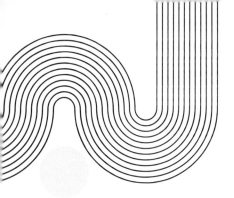

"When we are firmly grounded in our ventral vagal pathway, we feel safe and connected, calm and social."

Ventral energy nourishes our nervous systems. The more we notice and name ventral experiences, the more easily we can access ventral as a resource.

Imagine your ventral state as a container you can fill. Play with shapes and images and find the container that feels right to you. Reflect on your day and notice what you did that fills your container. How full is it? What is it about the experiences that felt nourishing?

Taking a step further: Draw a series of containers and engage in an end-of-the-day reflection for a week. Are there experiences that regularly fill your container? Look back at your week and notice how full your container was each day.

"Connecting with others is a universally beneficial experience but the ways we benefit from connection are individually created."

Connection is at the heart of well-being. Connecting with others is an essential part of living a life with health, purpose, ease, and joy.

Recall a moment of ventral connection with another person. What are the signs that let you know you were connecting? Cues might be body sensation, a sense of ease or calm, a feeling of being welcomed and not judged, a conversation that felt easy, or a sense of joining. Is there a way to share with this person your appreciation for the moment of connection? A note of thanks? A gesture of gratitude?

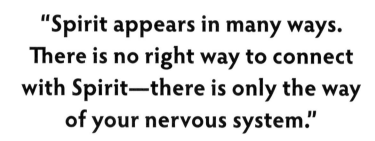

"Spirit appears in many ways.
There is no right way to connect
with Spirit—there is only the way
of your nervous system."

Connection with Spirit is an intimate, internal experience that often

comes with a feeling of grace. We may be deeply connected with

Spirit or still searching, but when we are filled with the energy of a

ventral state, the pathway to connection with Spirit is available.

What does Spirit mean to you? Notice the ways you connect to the energy of Spirit. You might find Spirit in nature, through spiritual beings, ancestral connections, or formal religious experiences. Reflect on the practices in your life that honor your connection to Spirit. Consider what other ways you might want to invite a connection.

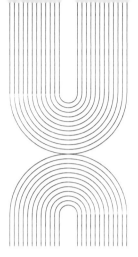

"Simply stopping during the day to take a moment just to be with yourself, to briefly turn inward and listen, builds those pathways of connection."

A part of feeling connected is connecting inside with a deep knowing of ourselves. Survival states bring self-criticism and self-blame, while our ventral state allows us to easily tune in and enjoy moments of connection.

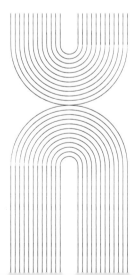

What are the activities, practices, or rituals that allow you to feel safely connected to self? This could be an activity that you enjoy, like reading, listening to your favorite music, or a hobby. It could be time spent meditating, cooking, or being out in nature. Set an intention to bring more of these opportunities into your life this week.

Taking it a step further: Put the intention into action with a plan. What are the specific steps you can take to support your intention? What can you do differently to facilitate this? List three steps you can take to deepen your connection to yourself this week. At the end of the week, come back and reflect on this experience.

"We come into the world wired for connection, one autonomic nervous system reaching out to another."

Nervous system to nervous system, we are all connected. When we are anchored in ventral, we feel a part of the human community and are open to compassionate connection.

What are the activities, actions, and events that allow you to feel connected to the world and feel a sense of common humanity? Review your week and notice the moments when you felt this kind of connection. How can you cultivate more of this?

Taking it a step further: Take an action this week that allows you to be purposeful in fostering this sense of connection. Perhaps you can spend some time in a public place, noticing the feeling of being surrounded by other nervous systems. Maybe there is an opportunity to volunteer in a helping pursuit that feeds your compassion and sense of connection. Maybe you can spend some time learning more about a global topic that speaks to you. Find the activity that feels right for you and reflect on the sense of connection that emerges.

"We all have a home in ventral safety and connection."

Wired into the autonomic nervous system of every human is a ventral vagal circuit. When we know what brings us home to ventral, we can begin to intentionally bring these moments to life.

Use your imagination to explore inviting more ventral experiences in your life. Make a list of things that would make up a ventral-inspired day. Rather than limiting your list to what might seem reasonable, put everything that you imagine on your list. Choose a couple of things from your list and plan a ventral-inspired day. At the end of the day, reflect on the experience. Keep planning days that bring things from your list into action.

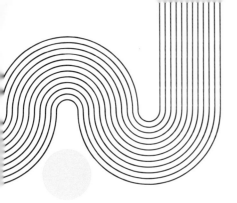

"Change is not an event but rather a lifelong process and autonomic reorganization is ongoing."

Our everyday actions affect our autonomic nervous system states. What we do in our day-to-day routines can support an ongoing experience of ventral or disrupt it.

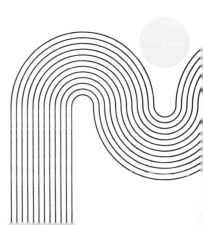

What are some ways your bedtime routine supports ventral vagal energy? What are some changes you can make to better honor your nervous system during this time?

Taking it a step further: Practice some of these routines regularly throughout the week and notice what happens when you intentionally support regulation through your bedtime routines. How does your sleep quality change? Does the time when you go to sleep or wake up change at all? Is there a shift in the energy you have at night, in the morning, or throughout the day when you bring intention to this routine?

"Habitual autonomic patterns work in the background, bringing a familiar rhythm to our everyday experiences. When those patterns are anchored in a flexible autonomic nervous system, ventral energy supports our ability to safely and successfully meet challenges and move through the day. This is a rhythm to deepen and celebrate."

Maintaining ventral regulation takes awareness of our choices and intentionality in our actions. By attending to the actions that bring our ventral state to life, we can create the conditions that support staying anchored in regulation.

Reflect on how you wake up and start the day. It is much easier to maintain ventral throughout your day if you can start there when your day begins. Does your current morning routine set you up to start your day in ventral? What are the steps in your routine that keep you anchored there? What are some changes you can make to better honor your nervous system?

Taking it a step further: Imagine you have 15 extra minutes each morning to support your morning routine. How would you spend this time? What else would you incorporate?

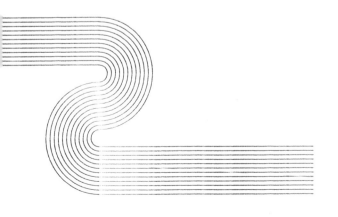

"Each autonomic state holds within it a multitude of flavors. Ventral is more than regulated and calm. It also brings joy, passion, excitement, celebration, interest, forthrightness, alertness, ease, and rest."

Ventral is the state where our bodies are in balance, we have access to empathy and compassion, we experience hope and possibilities, and we have a general sense of peace and well-being. When we are filled with ventral energy, we are regulated and ready to meet the day.

The ventral state of safety and connection contributes to your physical and emotional well-being. It works to regulate your nervous system and help you feel nourished as you navigate the day. Reflect on the ways your ventral system has served you today, and write a few words of appreciation.

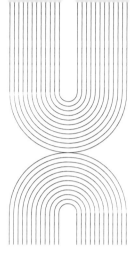

"As we integrate new patterns, we move out of our old stories and head toward new ones."

The autonomic nervous system is continuously being shaped by experience. Our nervous system is always seeking a path to regulation. With intention and regular practice, we have the capacity to reshape our nervous systems toward connection and well-being.

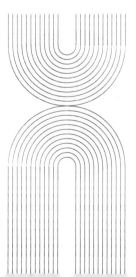

What wish do you have for your autonomic journey? What have you discovered so far that you want to strengthen? What are some habits you would like to change?

"Well-being is found in a balance of time with others and time by ourselves."

We are inherently social beings, and yet we also need time by ourselves. Some of us spend more time cozied up in safe solitude, while others feel most alive when surrounded by the buzz of other nervous systems. Throughout our lives, we travel between these two experiences—between solitude and social.

When do you feel the most social and externally engaged? What type of environment is ideal when you're feeling highly social? Who do you picture being there? How many people is too many? Now visualize being safe and cozy by yourself, filled with ventral energy. What do you imagine? Where are you? What elements add to your sense of safety?

Taking it a step further: Imagine you are in the company of a trusted loved one. What do you notice in your nervous system as you imagine this one-on-one time? Expand your vision to include a couple close friends or family members. Where does your system go? How does your sense of ventral energy change as you add more people to the experience? Now imagine yourself surrounded by many people that you know and love. What happens in your nervous system? If you imagine yourself surrounded by people that you don't know, what happens in your nervous system response then? Does this thought bring safe mobilization to your system? Or perhaps pull you into sympathetic activation? Go back to the image that brought you the most ventral vagal energy. Settle into this experience and savor the ventral energy it brings.

"Every nervous system is created with a ventral vagal pathway. Our biology includes this wired-in pathway of safety and connection. No matter how challenging our lives are, we can come home to safety."

Solitude is a regulating and nourishing experience of choosing to be alone and feeling a sense of peace in that aloneness. Having a sense of connection does not always mean we are surrounded by other people. A moment of solitude creates an experience of feeling centered and present.

Where in your environment can you find a place of solitude? Look for places where you feel a sense of connection to self, world, or Spirit when you are on your own. Find your way to those places and experiment with how much time there meets your need for solitude.

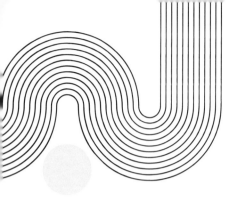

"With a greater capacity for staying anchored in ventral regulation and the ability to find the way back more easily to regulation from our states of dysregulation, we discover we have an expanded ability to feel safe and connect to the inherent wisdom of the autonomic nervous system."

Often, events that are unexpected and unfamiliar land as a cue of danger to our nervous system. There are times, however, when instead of a fear response, moments that are unexpected and unfamiliar bring a sense of excitement and anticipation. In these moments, rather than feeling the rise of survival energy, we are ready for an adventure.

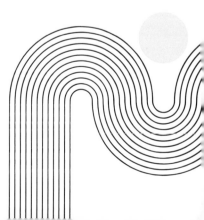

What did you encounter during your day that unexpectedly brought you a moment of excitement? Notice what was unfamiliar or unpredictable about the experience and reflect on the ways you stayed anchored in ventral. What were the resources that helped you feel safe enough to hold onto regulation?

"When we find our way to stillness, we discover comfort in moments of quiet, gather information from self-reflection, join with others in wordless connection, and are present to the joy of intimate experiences."

Stillness is a complex nervous system experience. It is a combination of quiet and connection that can be challenging to achieve. A moment of stillness in a busy day nourishes the nervous system.

How does stillness feel to you? How do you notice the difference between being safely still and disappearing into dorsal disconnection? Explore ways to move into safe stillness, allowing everything to slow down while staying present and holding on to your sense of safety. See if you can ease into stillness, slow your breath, and settle into a place of quiet for a moment.

Taking it a step further: Find a stillness activity that feels right for you. It could be doing a guided meditation, petting a beloved cat or dog in your life, spending some time focusing on a nearby tree or garden, or just mindfully watching your breath. Use this activity to enter moments of stillness throughout a day or week. Return and reflect on what the experience was like for you. When was it easier? When was it harder? Choose another stillness activity and explore for another day or week.

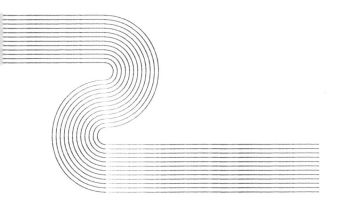

"When we partner with our autonomic nervous system, we can recruit the power of the system to help us navigate our days differently and write new stories of safety and connection."

When we find our way out of survival responses into a foundation of ventral regulation, we feel the solidity of this state of safety and connection, and hear a story of abundance.

When you think of a life rich with ventral abundance, what do you think of? What are some steps that you can take to work toward this vision?

Taking it a step further: Create a vision board. Use whatever materials you want to create a vision board that represents a life of ventral abundance. You might use pictures pulled from the internet, magazine cutouts, words, colors, materials from nature—the possibilities are endless.

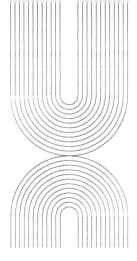

"When we learn to mindfully meet our nervous system, bring compassion to our embodied experiences, and honor our autonomic response, we have begun to befriend our nervous system."

Our nervous systems were created in service of survival. The practice of befriending is learning to tune in and turn toward our autonomic state and story with self-compassion. When we learn to befriend, we learn to appreciate the adaptive, protective qualities our survival states bring.

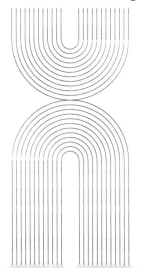

Write a few words of appreciation for the protection offered by your sympathetic state.

Write a few words of appreciation for the protection offered by your dorsal vagal state.

"As our ventral, sympathetic, and dorsal energies ebb and flow, how we experience the world changes."

Our states move in relationship with each other. As we experience life's challenges and life's joys, our nervous system states dance together, weaving together the story of our day. With enough safety, ventral can be the state in the foreground, guiding us toward connection and ease. With cues of danger present, sympathetic or dorsal may be in the foreground, protecting us with mobilized energy, or immobilization and collapse.

Notice what state is in the foreground for you right now. Feel that energy guiding your experience. Then tune into what state is in the background. What is the present-moment dance of your autonomic nervous system?

"While we are serious beings, problem-solvers wanting to make sense of the world, we are also playful beings wanting to let go of our problems for a moment in time."

Play engages both our ventral and sympathetic systems, allowing us to mobilize without losing our sense of connection and safety. While we may think play is a luxury, in fact being playful is a quality that contributes to well-being. When we attend to play, we can discover who we are as playful people.

How easy is it for you to play? What people, places, and experiences invite you to play? Notice any playful moments you've recently had. Make a list of ways you could invite more play into your daily experience.

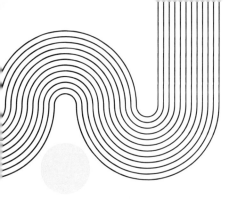

"Imagine you're an autonomic explorer learning about your nervous system."

When we step out of the activity that is around us and tune into our inner world, we come into connection with our autonomic experiences. Revisiting a place that was filled with safety and connection through imagination can bring us back to the moment and fill us with ventral energy. The experience is wired into our autonomic memory, and we relive it as we remember.

What is a favorite space that brings ventral regulation? Can you imagine yourself there? What sensations do you feel? What do you hear? What do you see? What do you feel? What is a thought that you have when you imagine yourself there?

"When we are firmly anchored in the ventral state, we feel truly embodied, present, safe, and ready to engage. Our brain adds information to help us engage with the world in an organized and resourceful way."

Flow is an experience of being in the zone, exploring a meaningful project, feeling calm, focused, passionate, and working with purpose.

In a flow state, you are fully immersed in the energy of ventral. What are some projects you are working on that bring you into flow? What are the qualities of those that invite a flow state (environment, coworkers, kind of project)? How might you invite more flow into your life?

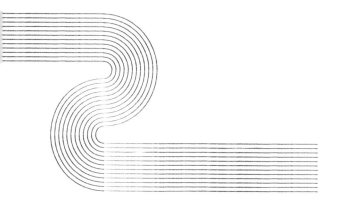

"Resilience helps us stay hopeful when things feel hopeless, engage an effective survival response in the face of danger, manage levels of stress in an ongoing stressful environment, and keep moving forward when the world around us is filled with suffering."

A flexible nervous system is a resilient system. Each time we move out of regulation and find the way back to ventral, we increase our capacity for flexibility and build our resilience.

Explore what resilience means to you by creating your personal resilience acronym. The following is an example of a resilience acronym. Choose your own words and create an acronym that illustrates the qualities of resilience that are important to you.

R: relaxed
E: energized
S: safe
I: invigorated
L: lighthearted
I: in tune
E: empathetic
N: navigating
C: calm
E: engaged

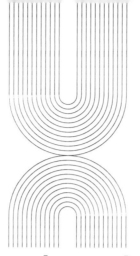

"In any building design, the foundation is the most important element. It is the ground upon which the structure rests. For humans, safety is the foundation. When the autonomic nervous system senses safety, the footings are deep and secure. When the system senses danger, the ground feels shaky."

When we can predictably experience cues of safety and bring them into explicit awareness, we reshape our response patterns to match the moment. Detecting and responding to cues of safety increases our capacity to move through the day with regulation.

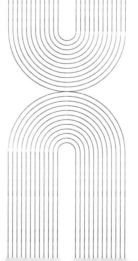

What cues of safety are present for you at this moment? Make a list of everything, big and small. Tune in and notice the cues of safety you feel inside yourself. Tune into your immediate surroundings, and notice what brings your system a sense of safety? Expand your awareness to include a larger space, perhaps the building you are in or the neighborhood around you. Reflect on your list and take in all the ways you are held in safety.

Taking it a step further: Take this practice out into the world. Go for a walk and bring your awareness to all the things that bring a sense of safety to your system. What do you notice?

"Within a co-regulated relationship, our quest for safety is realized, and we find sanctuary in the co-created experience of connection."

We depend on certain people in our lives that we reach out to when we are struggling and share our moments of joy. These connections are an essential ingredient for living a life of well-being.

Think of someone in your life who brings a sense of ease and safety when you think of them. What are some ways that you can create more connection with this person? Was there an opportunity to connect with them today? In person or in spirit? What could you do in the next day, week, month, and year to foster a stronger sense of connection? Create an intention to increase your connection with this person.

Taking it a step further: If this person is no longer alive, you might write them a letter or a note, or imagine talking with them. For someone who is still living, send them a text or an email, give them a call, give them a big hug, or even just imagine connecting with them. What do you notice in your system? How does your sense of connection shift when you take this extra step?

"The pathways to safety are wired into your biology and are waiting for you."

Our biology is wired with pathways to calm and connection. While we may not have traveled those pathways as often as we wish and may find them challenging to predictably hold on to, when we repeat small things to resource regulation, we strengthen our capacity to anchor in ventral.

What is a simple action that brings you a sense of ventral safety and connection that can serve as an anchor? Look for something that isn't a big practice that takes you out of the flow of your day but is easy to do and incorporate into your daily experiences. Once you have a list of actions, look for opportunities to use them to reach for regulation.

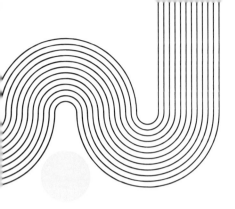

"Reciprocity is the mutual ebb and flow that defines nourishing relationships."

Reciprocity is an important regulator of our nervous systems. It is a connection between people that is created in the back-and-forth communication between two nervous systems. Through reciprocal regulation of our autonomic states, we feel safe to move into connection and create trusting relationships.

Who is a safe person in your life you feel connected to? What are the qualities of this relationship that make it safe? What does this person do that invites you in?

Taking it a step further: Reflect on what you are offering in your relationships. Are you offering the qualities you identified are important for you to receive from others? What are some actions you can take to be a source of connection and support to others the way they are for you?

"We depend on the vagal brake's capacity to relax and reengage as we navigate the demands of a normal day."

The vagal brake allows us to quickly energize and then return to calm. It is there to give us the energy we need to successfully meet a moment from a place of ventral safety. With an efficiently functioning vagal brake, we transition between experiences with ease.

Imagine a mechanism that can represent your vagal brake. Look for something you can control to increase and decrease the output of energy. It might be a water faucet, bicycle brakes, a dimmer switch, a window that can open and close. Let your imagination guide you. Draw your symbol. Play with the motion that might go along with this mechanism. When you have a sense of your vagal brake image and motion managing your energy flow, travel back to your experiences from the day. Adjust your vagal brake to find just the right amount of energy that you needed to navigate those moments.

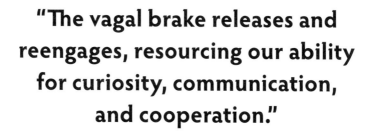

"The vagal brake releases and reengages, resourcing our ability for curiosity, communication, and cooperation."

When we relax our vagal brake, we allow sympathetic energy to increase to help us meet a challenge, without going into fight or flight. When we reengage our brake, we reduce the amount of sympathetic energy in our system and bring in more calm.

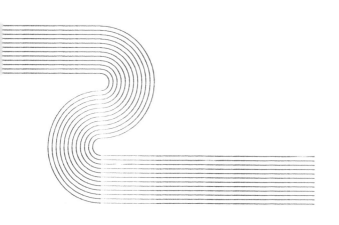

Take a moment to reflect on times during the day when you needed a boost of energy and times when you needed calm. Appreciate the ways your vagal brake helped you successfully manage the moments. Is there an upcoming event that you anticipate will activate your sympathetic survival system? Use the image and movement you created for your vagal brake and visualize it working to help you meet the challenge.

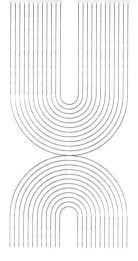

"The process of looking at what stretches and what stresses our system is a way to create just the right degree of challenge to invite in new patterns and deepen ones that are already working."

To reshape our system, we need to create experiences that give our autonomic nervous systems evidence that even though something feels a bit scary, we can in fact handle it and stay safe and regulated.

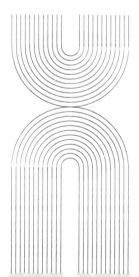

Can you identify areas in your life where you are safe to stretch a bit?
What are the cues of safety that tell you it's safe to try? Is there a way you
might intentionally stretch your system this week? Perhaps it means reaching
out to someone with whom you have a strained relationship. Perhaps there is a
difficult conversation you need to have. Maybe there is a decision to be made
that feels a little risky but you know will be manageable for you in the end.
Intentionally take a step to stretch your system and reflect on the experience.

"Learning to listen to the wisdom of the autonomic nervous system and honoring the right degree of challenge is the foundation for change."

Rather than powering through an experience and stressing our system, we can create the right degree of challenge to invite in new patterns. When we engage in actions that shape our system in new ways while we are still holding on to our anchor in the ventral state, we can stretch, feel the shape of a new pattern, and step into the process of change.

What is something that you have been wanting to change and have been avoiding? What state is activated when you think about that? If your system responded with some sympathetic or dorsal activation, something feels a bit unsafe. Let's honor the nervous system and discover what you might need to stay anchored in ventral vagal and move forward. Identify a small step related to this pursuit that allows you to move forward with a sense of safety. If your system still responds with an activated survival response, try one step smaller and see what shifts. When you've identified a step that feels safe enough, take this small step this week, and reflect on that experience.

"**We are living a story that originates in our autonomic state, is sent through autonomic pathways from the body to the brain, and is then translated by the brain into the beliefs that guide our daily experience.**"

Our nervous system takes in information through neuroception and then moves us in and out of regulation. Our brain's job is to make sense of the ways this happens by creating a story. We then enter that story and believe it to be true. If we can remember there are three states, each with its own narrative, we can begin to see beyond one storyline.

Reflect on a recent event when you were pulled into a survival state.
Which survival state was activated? What was the corresponding story?
Consider your other survival state and the story that is created from that
energy. Find the way to ventral and listen to the story from this place of
regulation. What were the messages from each of your states?

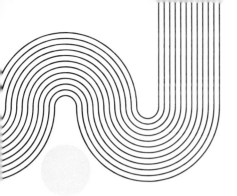

"[I can] move out of the self-critical story of who I am into curiosity about how I respond."

We all have inner critics that emerge from our survival states. When we bring ventral regulation to hearing the stories our critics bring, we begin to understand what the protective purpose might be. Looking through the lens of ventral, we can bring curiosity and compassion to our story, and challenge some of the messages that come from a survival state.

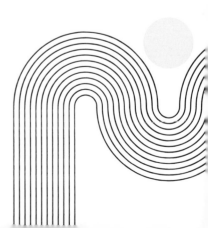

Reflect on the messages you hear from your inner critics. Listen to the ones that are coming from sympathetic anger and anxiety and the ones that are coming from dorsal hopelessness. What are some common messages you hear from these states, about yourself and about the world? When you add ventral energy to these messages, what changes?

"Humans are meaning-making beings, automatically pulled toward story."

From an anchor in ventral, we can stay out of judgment and self-criticism and explore our stories with curiosity and compassion. Rather than being pulled into an old story, we can access our inner observer and see our stories in a new way.

Get to know your inner observer. What does it look like? How does it show up for you? If you could meet and talk, what would you want to know? Imagine having that conversation.

Taking it a step further: From a place of connection with your inner observer, you can experience yourself with curiosity and compassion, watching your stories instead of being caught in them. Inner critics come from survival states and bring messages that match the state they come from. What might your inner observer say about the stories that come from your inner critics?

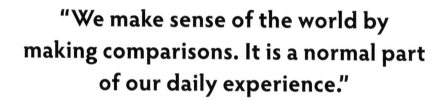

"We make sense of the world by making comparisons. It is a normal part of our daily experience."

To compare is to be human. We have comparing stories that emerge

from our survival states and ones that are held in regulation.

Comparing activates autonomic states, and with those come

stories of disconnection and connection.

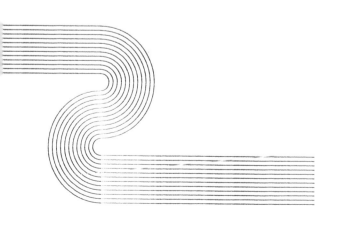

When you are pulled into a survival state, you sometimes feel better than others and sometimes not as good as others. Reflect on moments when you were pulled into each of your survival states and notice the messages you hear. Then consider what the message would be from a ventral state in those moments of comparison. Write a ventral letter to yourself, noting the ways that you are, in fact, okay as you are. From a ventral place, tell yourself all the things that are hard to access from a survival state. Harness the emergent properties of ventral as you write—flexibility, compassion, connection, kindness, love, and hope.

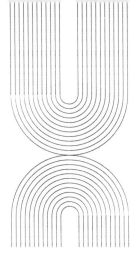

"As we learn that our nervous system works in accordance with the same survival systems all humans share, we begin to make space for self-compassion."

Seeing the world through the lens of our nervous systems has the potential to create a dramatic shift in how we show up in the world. We can understand others with curiosity and compassion, knowing everybody has a nervous system that responds in service of survival.

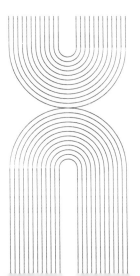

When you are regulated, you can be intentional in the messages you are broadcasting to the world and offer ventral vagal energy to those around you. What has this shift been like for you as you have continued to deepen your practice of embodied awareness?

"We are all on an autonomic journey—an adventure that includes survival and safety, protection and connection."

The normal rhythm of our daily life moves us in and out of regulation. We regularly travel from ventral safety to moments of sympathetic and dorsal survival and return to regulation. Getting to know the ways our states work on their own and in relationship with each other helps us understand, and even shape, our autonomic journey.

Choose an object to represent your sympathetic and dorsal survival states and ventral regulation. Notice what drew you to each object. Write a story for each object, sharing what it is about each object that guided your choice. Arrange your objects in different ways to experiment with the different experiences of regulation and survival. Reflect on what you experience.

"The autonomic nervous system has an inherent longing to be in ventral . . . and an inherent knowing about how to get there."

Every human has a ventral state, and the pathways to regulation are wired into our biology. Certain objects remind us of the predictable presence of ventral energy in our lives and our ability to reach for that connection.

Find a small object that you can carry around with you that represents your ventral state and helps you connect and feel held there. Place it somewhere where you are likely to encounter it during the day—maybe in your pocket or next to your computer. What is it like to have this small, tangible reminder of your ventral capacity throughout the day?

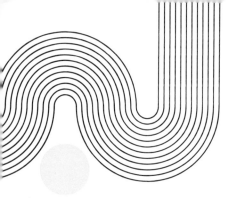

"Touch can activate our survival responses or help us anchor in safety."

Touch can bring a safe return of sensation when our body feels numb, create connection to the present when we feel lost, calm our system when we are distressed, and bring us home to regulation and help us anchor there.

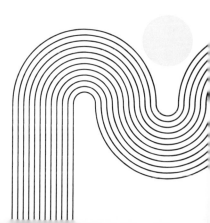

What are some types of self-touch that feel safe to you and some types that typically activate a survival response? Try various kinds of self-touch and notice how your nervous system responds. Try placing your hand on the top of your head. Place your hands on the sides of your face. Cup your jaw. Wrap your arms around your chest and give yourself a hug. Tug on your earlobes. Place a hand on your heart, the small of your back, your abdomen, your knees. Try different motions, such as tapping or applying pressure. Make a list of what feels resourcing.

"Our brain and body are intimately connected, autonomic state and psychological story forming experiences and expectations that are sometimes nourishing and sometimes painful. Through the art of reflection we have the power to shape our systems in the direction of safety and connection."

Our survival states work to help us be safe in the world. In the beginning, survival energy was on its own, acting to keep us safe. With time and experience, we learn to bring ventral connection to those old pathways, and then we can use the old actions in a new way.

Think about your survival energy tempered with ventral connection and imagine this as your autonomic superpower. What would it be, and how does it work? Maybe you have harnessed chaotic sympathetic energy into passion for your purpose in life, or shifted old patterns of dorsal shutdown into creativity that emerges from times of being quiet. Reflect on the ways your superpower moves you forward. Now reflect on times when your superpower came to your rescue. Remember a time when a flood of sympathetic energy was moderated by ventral regulation and you spoke up, or a time when dorsal collapse was influenced by ventral and you disconnected from the challenges around you to find a moment of safety. Take a moment to appreciate the amazing ways you have learned to use the inherent wisdom and power of your autonomic nervous system to navigate life in new ways, reach your goals, and make a difference in the world.

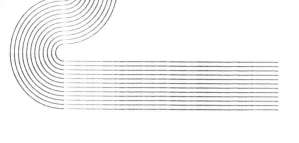

"Awe brings a sense of wonder. It challenges our ordinary ways of thinking. For a moment, we step out of ourselves and our usual ways of being in the world."

Awe is found in extraordinary moments. We encounter something that stops us in our tracks, a moment so awe-inspiring that we are awestruck. Awe is also found in everyday experiences: a bird singing, a flower blooming in the garden, a piece of music playing. Moments of awe are abundant in our everyday world and are truly an autonomic experience.

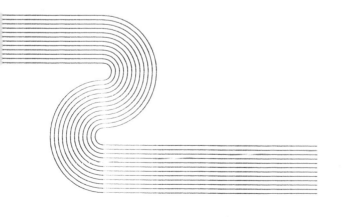

Think about the ways awe appeared in your day. Awe may happen in big, dramatic ways, or small micromoments of joy. Write about or illustrate a moment of awe you discovered today.

Taking it a step further: Engage in this practice for several weeks. Review your writing or illustrations and look for any predictable places and times that awe appeared.

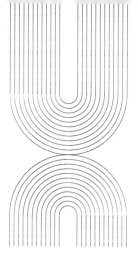

"Awe is a state of wonder, curiosity, reverence, and deep appreciation. It exists along a continuum of ordinary to extraordinary, from everyday moments that are awe-inspiring to the profound moments when we are awestruck."

A moment of awe brings a sense of wonder. We feel both small and connected to something much larger than ourselves, and our old way of thinking no longer fits. We experience awe in both extraordinary and ordinary moments and can deepen our sense of well-being by learning to notice the everyday moments of awe all around us.

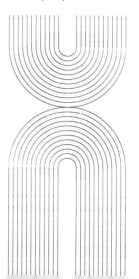

Look for everyday awe experiences. Art, music, and the natural world regularly offer moments of awe. Get to know the cues from your body and mind that you are experiencing a moment of everyday awe. Set an intention to watch for ordinary moments of awe as you move through your daily routine.

Taking it a step further: Though awe is an experience that is uniquely your own, when you share your experience of awe with another person the experience often deepens and brings a sense of connection. Share your experience of a moment of awe with a safe person in your life and notice what changes.

A BEGINNER'S GUIDE TO POLYVAGAL THEORY

We come into the world wired to connect. With our first breath, we embark on a lifelong quest to feel safe in our bodies, in our environments, and in our relationships with others. The autonomic nervous system is our personal surveillance system, always on guard, asking the question, "Is this safe?" Its goal is to protect us by sensing safety and risk, listening moment by moment to what is happening in and around our bodies and in the connections we have to others. This listening happens far below awareness and far away from our conscious control. Dr. Porges, understanding that this is not awareness that comes with perception, coined the term *neuroception* to describe the way our autonomic nervous system scans for cues of safety, danger, and life threat without involving the thinking parts of our brain. Because we humans are meaning-making beings, what begins as the wordless experiencing of neuroception drives the creation of a story that shapes our daily living.

The Autonomic Nervous System

The autonomic nervous system is made up of two main branches, the sympathetic and the parasympathetic, and responds to signals and sensations via three pathways, each with a characteristic pattern of response. Through each of these pathways, we react in service of survival.

The sympathetic branch is found in the middle part of the spinal cord and represents the pathway that prepares us for action. It responds to cues of danger and triggers the release of adrenaline, which fuels the fight-or-flight response.

In the parasympathetic branch, Polyvagal Theory focuses on two pathways traveling within a nerve called the vagus. Vagus, meaning "wanderer," is aptly named. From the brain stem at the base of the skull, the vagus travels in two directions: downward through the lungs, heart, diaphragm, and stomach and upward to connect with nerves in the neck, throat, eyes, and ears. The vagus is divided into two parts: the ventral vagal pathway and the dorsal vagal pathway. The ventral vagal pathway responds to cues of safety and supports feelings of being safely engaged and socially connected. In contrast, the dorsal vagal pathway responds to cues of extreme danger. It takes us out of connection, out of awareness, and into a protective state of collapse. When we feel collapsed, numb, or not here, the dorsal vagus has taken control.

Dr. Porges identified a hierarchy of response built into our autonomic nervous system and anchored in the evolutionary development of our species. The origin of the dorsal vagal pathway of the parasympathetic branch and its immobilization response lies with our ancient vertebrate ancestors and is the oldest pathway. The sympathetic branch and its pattern of mobilization was next to develop. The most recent addition, the ventral vagal pathway of the parasympathetic branch, brings patterns of social engagement that are unique to mammals.

When we are firmly grounded in our ventral vagal pathway, we feel safe and connected, calm and social. A sense (neuroception) of danger can trigger us out of this state and backward on the evolutionary timeline into the sympathetic branch. Here we are mobilized to respond and take action. Taking action can help us return to the safe and social state. It is when we feel as though we are trapped and can't escape the danger that the dorsal vagal pathway pulls us all the way back to our evolutionary beginnings. In this state we are immobilized. We shut down to survive. From here, it is a long way back to feeling safe and social, and a painful path to follow.

The Autonomic Ladder

Let's translate our basic knowledge of the autonomic nervous system into everyday understanding by imagining the autonomic nervous system as a ladder. How do our experiences change as we move down and back up the ladder?

The Top of the Ladder Safety and connection are guided by the evolutionarily newest part of the autonomic nervous system. Our social engagement system is active in the ventral vagal pathway of the parasympathetic branch. In this state, our heart rate is regulated, our breath is full, we take in the faces of friends, we can tune in to conversations and tune out distracting noises. We see the big picture and connect to the world and the people in it. I might describe myself as happy, active, and interested and the world as safe, fun, and peaceful. From this ventral vagal place at the top of the autonomic ladder, I am connected to myself and can reach out to others. Some of the daily living experiences of this state include being organized, following through with plans, taking care of myself, taking time to play, doing things with others, feeling productive at work, and having a general feeling of regulation and a sense of management. Health benefits include a healthy heart, regulated blood pressure, a healthy immune system decreasing my vulnerability to illness, good digestion, quality sleep, and an overall sense of well-being.

Moving Down the Ladder The sympathetic branch of the autonomic nervous system activates when we feel a stirring of unease—when something triggers a neuroception of danger. We go into action. Fight or flight happens here. In this state, our heart rate speeds up, our breath is short and shallow, we scan our environment looking for danger—we are on the move. I might describe myself as anxious or angry and feel the rush of adrenaline that makes it hard for me to be still. I am listening for sounds of danger and don't hear the sounds of friendly voices. The world may feel dangerous, chaotic, and unfriendly. From this place of sympathetic mobilization—a step down the autonomic ladder and backward on the evolutionary timeline—I may believe, "The world is a dangerous place and I need to protect myself from harm." Some of the daily living problems can be anxiety, panic attacks, anger, inability to focus or follow through, and distress in relationships. Health consequences can include heart disease, high blood pressure, high cholesterol, sleep problems, weight gain, memory impairment, headache, chronic neck, shoulder, and back tension, stomach problems, and increased vulnerability to illness.

The Bottom of the Ladder Our oldest pathway of response, the dorsal vagal pathway of the parasympathetic branch, is the path of last resort. When all else fails, when we are trapped and taking action doesn't work, the primitive vagus takes us into shutdown, collapse, and dissociation. Here at the very bottom of the autonomic ladder, I am alone with my despair and escape into not knowing, not feeling, almost a sense of not being. I might describe myself as hopeless, abandoned, foggy, too tired to think or act, and the world as empty, dead, and dark. From this earliest place on the evolutionary timeline, where my mind and body have moved into conservation mode, I may believe, "I am lost and no one will ever find me." Some of the daily living problems can be dissociation, problems with memory, depression, isolation, and no energy for the tasks of daily living. Health consequences of this state can include chronic fatigue, fibromyalgia, stomach problems, low blood pressure, Type 2 diabetes, and weight gain.

Moving on the Ladder

Now that we've explored each of the places on the autonomic ladder, let's consider how we move up and down. Our preferred place is at the top of the ladder. The ventral vagal state is hopeful and resourceful. We can live, love, and laugh by ourselves and with others. This is not a place where everything is wonderful or a place without problems. But it is a place where we have the ability to acknowledge distress and explore options, to reach out for support and develop organized responses. We move down the ladder into action when we are triggered into a sense of unease—of impending danger. We hope that our action taking here will give us enough space to take a breath and climb back up the ladder to the place of safety and connection. It is when we fall all the way down to the bottom rungs that the safety and hope at the top of the ladder feel unreachable.

Systems Working Together

We experience well-being when the three parts of our autonomic nervous system work together. To understand this integration, we leave the imagery of the ladder and imagine instead a home. The dorsal vagal system runs the basic utilities of the home. This system works continually in the background, keeping our basic body systems online and in order. When there is a glitch in the system, we pay attention. When all is running smoothly, the body's functions work automatically. Without the influence of the ventral vagal system, the basic utilities run the empty house, but no one is home. Or, if we are home, the environment is one that brings no comfort. Everything is turned down to the lowest possible setting—enough to keep the air circulating and the pipes from freezing. The environment is just habitable enough to sustain life. The sympathetic branch can be thought of as the home security system, maintaining a range of responses and armed to react to any emergencies. This alarm system is designed to trigger an immediate response and then return to standby. Without the influence of the ventral vagal system, the alarm system receives a steady stream of emergency notifications and continues to sound the alarm. The ventral vagal system allows us to soak in, and savor, this home we are inhabiting. We can enjoy it as a place to rest and renew by ourselves and as a place to join with friends and family. We feel the basic utilities running in the background. The rhythms of our heart and breath are regulated. We trust that the monitoring system is on standby. The integration of systems allows us to be compassionate, curious about the world we live in, and emotionally and physically connected to the people around us.

Where Do We Go Next?

This Beginner's Guide is written to offer an understanding of the autonomic nervous system's role and responses in service of our safety and survival. With this knowledge, we can begin to befriend the autonomic nervous system and map our personal response patterns. The befriending skills lead to attending practices. Our mapping leads naturally to tracking. With the awareness of tracking, we can begin to intentionally tune and tone our autonomic nervous system. We can successfully navigate our quest for safety and connection.

GLOSSARY

Hierarchy

The autonomic nervous system responds to sensations in the body and signals from the environment through three pathways of response. These pathways work in a specified order and respond to challenges in predictable ways. The three pathways (and their patterns of response), in evolutionary order from oldest to newest, are the dorsal vagus (immobilization), the sympathetic nervous system (mobilization), and the ventral vagus (social engagement and connection). Each pathway brings its own set of thoughts, feelings, behaviors, and bodily experiences. Ventral, at the top of the autonomic hierarchy, is the system of connection. The ventral state is essential for health and well-being. In this state, we feel grounded, organized, and ready to meet the day. Life feels manageable; we see options, have hope, and hear new stories. We connect to ourselves, to others, to the world around us, and to Spirit. We are regulated and ready to engage. When a moment feels too big and overwhelms us, we move down one step on the hierarchy into the sympathetic system's fight and flight responses and are pulled into anxiety and anger. If this doesn't help, we land at the bottom of the hierarchy in dorsal vagal collapse. From the dorsal state, we feel drained, without enough energy to engage with the world. We collapse, disconnect, and disappear. We regularly travel this hierarchy as we navigate the challenges of daily living.

Neuroception

Coined by Polyvagal Theory developer Stephen Porges, the term *neuroception* describes how our autonomic nervous system takes in information. This inner, subconscious surveillance system gathers information through three pathways: within our bodies, in the world around us, and in our connections to others. Through neuroception, we are continuously broadcasting and receiving messages of welcome and warning. In response to the information we receive via neuroception, we move from state to state along the autonomic hierarchy.

Co-regulation

Co-regulation is an experience of two nervous systems attuning in safety and connection. Through the process of co-regulation, one person uses their ventral state to help another person find their way to regulation. Polyvagal Theory identifies co-regulation as a biological imperative: a need that must be met to sustain life. We are born needing to be cared for by others to ensure our survival. We are physically unable to regulate on our own and turn to the people around us to meet both our physical and emotional survival needs. As we grow, these experiences of co-regulation offer a foundation to explore self-regulation. Even as we learn to self-regulate, the need for co-regulation continues. Co-regulation is a necessary ingredient for physical and emotional well-being. Throughout our lives we look for—and long for—safe, reliable connections.

Social Engagement System

The social engagement system came into being in our evolutionary history when the ventral pathway to the heart and four pathways to the face and head formed a connection in the brain stem. This is both a sending and receiving system, continuously posting information about ourselves and gathering information about others. Each individual element of the social engagement system sends signals either inviting or discouraging connection and at the same time tunes into other social engagement systems looking for signs of warning or welcome. The elements of the social engagement system are essential to assessing safety and danger. Our eyes send signals of safety and look into other eyes for signs of welcome. Our ears tune in to conversations, listening for the sounds of friendship, while our tone of voice alerts others to the meaning underneath our words. Our facial expressions convey social information. Our shoulders move, our head turns and tilts, sending signals that we are safe to approach. When we sense looks, sounds, and gestures that invite connection, we move closer. Meeting looks, sounds, and gestures that send signals that we are unsafe, we move into watchfulness. We communicate, one nervous system to another, that it is safe to approach and come into relationship or that it's better to stay away. It is the social engagement system that orchestrates this autonomic experience.

Vagal Brake

The vagal brake is a particular pathway that begins in the brain stem and goes to the sinoatrial node of the heart, which is the heart's pacemaker. The vagal brake is responsible for speeding up and slowing down heart rate to effectively respond to the needs of the moment. The vagal pathway to the heart becomes more active or less active, relaxing and reengaging, using electrical signals and neurotransmitters. The vagal brake allows more of the sympathetic nervous system's energy to be felt while keeping the ventral vagal system online and in charge. As the vagal brake begins to relax, the energy flowing through the vagal pathway is reduced a bit, and the sympathetic energy that is in the background begins to move into the foreground. Then as the vagal brake reengages, the process is reversed, sympathetic moving to the background and ventral vagal back to the foreground. With the vagal brake relaxing but not fully releasing, we have access to a range of responses including feeling calm, engaged, joyful, excited, passionate, playful, attentive, alert, or watchful, while still safely situated in the ventral vagal system. The vagal brake allows us to rapidly engage and disengage, to quickly energize and return to calm in response to the demands of the moment. With a flexible vagal brake, we can be reflective and responsive rather than reactive. An efficiently functioning vagal brake brings the ability to rapidly engage and disengage, energize and calm, and experience ease in making these transitions.

Savor

To savor is to connect with, and deepen, the moments of ventral vagal regulation that inevitably emerge as we move through the day. This is an active strategy to build ventral vagal resources. Savoring is a quick practice that captures a ventral vagal moment and holds it in conscious attention for just a short time, making it easy to do during the natural flow of your day. A 20- to 30-second snapshot is all that is needed to benefit from the practice. Savoring is about seeing and celebrating the little things in everyday life. When we bring these moments into awareness and spend just a short amount of time actively engaged in attending to them, the benefits are both immediate, as we feel anchored in ventral safety, and longer term, with gains in physical and emotional well-being.

Three steps of savoring:

Attend: Notice a ventral micromoment (glimmer). Focus your attention on it.

Appreciate: Hold the moment in your awareness and appreciate its presence.

Amplify: Stay with the moment for 20–30 seconds and let it fill you.

Sometimes negative thoughts intrude and interrupt the ability to stay in the ventral experience and, rather than resourcing, the practice of savoring becomes distressing. It's not an uncommon experience to think we don't deserve to feel this, it's dangerous to feel good, or something bad will happen if we stop and appreciate the moment. When this happens, we can start slowly with five or 10 seconds of savoring, and build toward 20 or 30. Each micro-moment shapes our systems. Over time, the ability to savor will build to the 20–30 seconds that defines a savoring experience.

Autonomic Ladder

The autonomic ladder was created as a way to visualize the autonomic hierarchy in an easy-to-use format showing the three states in the predictable order we travel through them. The ladder image invites a sense of safe transitions. Moving down and up a ladder does not require a leap across a gap but instead involves a steady progression from rung to rung. A ladder is always in contact with the ground, offering a way to safely reach higher places. In this case, the ground for our ladder is the evolutionary root of dorsal vagal energy, and the transition upward takes us through the energized sympathetic state and into the ventral vagal state of social connection.

Ventral Vagal

Sympathetic

Dorsal Vagal

SOURCES

Prompts

2   "When we notice our autonomic experience, we have a chance to engage with it, not simply be engaged by it." —*Polyvagal Theory in Therapy*, p. 100

4   "Autonomic patterns are built over time. The autonomic nervous system is shaped by experience." —*Polyvagal Theory in Therapy*, p. 33

6   "Ventral vagal energy supports self-compassion—the act of reaching in to be with our own suffering with kindness. In a ventral state, hope arises, and change is possible." —*Polyvagal Theory in Therapy*, p. 27

8   "The reassuring, heartwarming news is that autonomic flexibility can be shaped over time." —*Polyvagal Theory in Therapy*, p. 122

10   "Being able to correctly identify autonomic states is the necessary first step in the process of shaping our system in a new way." —*Polyvagal Exercises for Safety in Connection*, p. 43

12   "Glimmers are the micro-moments of ventral vagal experience that routinely appear in everyday life yet frequently go unnoticed." —*Polyvagal Exercises for Safety in Connection*, p. 109

14   "Music is all around us, affecting our physiology and our feelings." —*Polyvagal Exercises for Safety in Connection*, p. 115

16   "Music is a gentle way to travel the hierarchy." —*Polyvagal Card Deck*

18   "Our brains say, 'we should' or 'of course' to make a quick decision, while our nervous systems use 'maybe' and 'what if' to invite a moment of contemplation." —*Polyvagal Practices*, p. 35

20   "How we move through the world—turning toward, backing away, sometimes connecting and other times isolating—is guided by the autonomic nervous system." —*Polyvagal Theory in Therapy*, p. 4

22   "We live a story that originates in our autonomic nervous system, is sent through autonomic pathways from the body to the brain, and is then translated by the brain into the beliefs that guide our daily living." —*Polyvagal Theory in Therapy*, p. 35

24   "Change involves leaning into a pattern that is nourishing and moving away from a pattern that is draining." —*Polyvagal Card Deck*

26   "When autonomic patterns begin to change, we find ourselves in the unfamiliar experience of being between—not held in old patterns and not yet predictably in new ones." —*Polyvagal Exercises for Safety in Connection*, p. 147

28   "We regularly travel the hierarchy as we navigate the challenges of daily living." —*Polyvagal Card Deck*

30 "With 18 breaths per minute, an adult takes 25,902 breaths a day . . . and in each of those breaths, there is an opportunity to shape the nervous system toward safety and connection." —*Polyvagal Theory in Therapy*, p. 134

32 "Glimmers offer a reminder that our nervous systems can hold both dysregulation and regulation—that our days can be filled with difficulty, and we can also feel a spark of ventral safety." —*Polyvagal Practices*, p. 89

34 "The autonomic nervous system responds to the challenges of daily living by telling us not what we are or who we are but how we are." —*Polyvagal Theory in Therapy*, p. 17

36 "Through understanding how the autonomic nervous system takes in embodied, environmental, and relational experiences, we become active operators of our systems and authors of our own autonomic stories." —*Polyvagal Practices*, p. 111

38 "Haiku captures a moment in time in just a few words." —*Polyvagal Card Deck*

40 "Autonomic state shifts in response to the challenges of daily life are a normal and expected experience. The goal is to not always be in a state of ventral regulation but rather to be able to flexibly navigate the small ordinary shifts that are a part of everyday life." —*Polyvagal Exercises for Safety in Connection*, p. 158

42 "Glimmers gently yet significantly shape our systems toward well-being. Once we learn to look for glimmers, we find they are all around us and we begin to look for more." —*Polyvagal Practices*, p. 89

44 "What our nervous system knows and will do to help us survive is quite amazing . . . and undeniable." —*Polyvagal Practices*, p. 36

46 "The autonomic nervous systems of two people find sanctuary in a co-created experience of connection." —*Polyvagal Theory in Therapy*, p. 44

48 "With the many moving pieces of people and connections that make up our lives, there is often a chaotic mix of autonomic energies. The goal is to navigate with flexibility." —*Polyvagal Theory in Therapy*, p. 50

50 "The autonomic nervous system is a common denominator in our human family." —*Polyvagal Theory in Therapy*, p. 17

52 "We can be surprised by the creativity of our internal world to bring our autonomic experiences to life." —*Anchored*, p. 61

54 "The autonomic nervous system is at the heart of our lived experience." —*Polyvagal Theory in Therapy*, p. 121

56 "Beneath the level of conscious awareness our nervous system directs our movement toward and away from people, places, and experiences." —*Polyvagal Theory in Therapy*, p. 119

58 "Human connections, necessary for survival, are nonetheless challenging, and moments of relationship messiness are common." —*Polyvagal Theory in Therapy*, p. 133

60 "There is no right or wrong way. There is just the way of your nervous system." —Foundations of Polyvagal Informed Practice Workshop

62 "We are social beings who also need times of solitude." —*Polyvagal Practices*, p. 27

64 "Through co-regulation we connect with others and create a shared sense of safety." —*Polyvagal Exercises for Safety in Connection*, p. 3

66 "I love the smell of the sea and pine trees. These are the smells of home for me. I light a scented candle and find my way to regulation." —*Anchored*, p. 94

68 "Glimmers are a reminder that ventral energy is always around waiting to be noticed and nourish our nervous systems." —*Polyvagal Practices*, p. 90

70 "To savor is to take a moment of ventral regulation and the feeling of safety and experience a story of connection." —*Polyvagal Exercises for Safety in Connection*, p. 97

72 "Glimmers build the foundation for our well-being." —*Polyvagal Exercises for Safety in Connection*, p. xxiv

74 "Autonomic regulation and a story of safety happen when the heart and the breath are in harmony." —*Polyvagal Exercises*, p. 124

76 "We can think about our moment-to-moment experience as an equation. Because the nervous system is always taking in cues, the safety/danger equation is always changing." —*Polyvagal Practices*, p. 42

78 "It is not enough to resolve cues of danger. We must also experience cues of safety." —*Polyvagal Theory in Therapy*, p. 67

80 "We come into the world wired to connect." —*Polyvagal Theory in Therapy*, p. 7

82 "Choice is an essential element for a regulated nervous system." —*Anchored*, p. 11

84 "With regular practice, our nervous system's capacity for flexibility is resourced." —*Polyvagal Practices*, p. 129

86 "Experiences in nature also bring the ventral state alive." —*Polyvagal Theory in Therapy*, p. 63

88 "Nature, both in real life and through viewing images, offers relaxing and restorative opportunities." —*Polyvagal Exercises for Safety in Connection*, p. 101

90 "When we are firmly grounded in our ventral vagal pathway, we feel safe and connected, calm and social." —*Polyvagal Theory in Therapy*, p. 9

92 "Connecting with others is a universally beneficial experience but the ways we benefit from connection are individually created." —*Polyvagal Exercises for Safety in Connection*, p. 175

94 "Spirit appears in many ways. There is no right way to connect with Spirit— there is only the way of your nervous system." —*Polyvagal Practices*, p. 58

96 "Simply stopping during the day to take a moment just to be with yourself, to briefly turn inward and listen, builds those pathways of connection." —*Anchored*, p. 45

98 "We come into the world wired for connection, one autonomic nervous sys-

tem reaching out to another." —*Polyvagal Exercises for Safety in Connection*, p. 170

100 "We all have a home in ventral safety and connection." —*Polyvagal Practices*, p. 31

102 "Change is not an event but rather a lifelong process and autonomic reorganization is ongoing." —*Polyvagal Practices*, p. 87

104 "Habitual autonomic patterns work in the background, bringing a familiar rhythm to our everyday experiences. When those patterns are anchored in a flexible autonomic nervous system, ventral energy supports our ability to safely and successfully meet challenges and move through the day. This is a rhythm to deepen and celebrate." —*Polyvagal Exercises for Safety in Connection*, p. 149

106 "Each autonomic state holds within it a multitude of flavors. Ventral is more than regulated and calm. It also brings joy, passion, excitement, celebration, interest, forthrightness, alertness, ease, and rest." —*Polyvagal Exercises for Safety in Connection*, p. 103

108 "As we integrate new patterns, we move out of our old stories and head toward new ones." —*Polyvagal Exercises for Safety in Connection*, p. 156

110 "Well-being is found in a balance of time with others and time by ourselves." —*Polyvagal Exercises for Safety in Connection*, p. 171

112 "Every nervous system is created with a ventral vagal pathway. Our biology includes this wired-in pathway of safety and connection. No matter how challenging our lives are, we can come home to safety." —*Polyvagal Practices*, p. 31

114 "With a greater capacity for staying anchored in ventral regulation and the ability to find the way back more easily to regulation from our states of dysregulation, we discover we have an expanded ability to feel safe and connect to the inherent wisdom of the autonomic nervous system." —*Polyvagal Practices*, p. 70

116 "When we find our way to stillness, we discover comfort in moments of quiet, gather information from self-reflection, join with others in wordless connection, and are present to the joy of intimate experiences." —*Polyvagal Practices*, p. 95

118 "When we partner with our autonomic nervous system, we can recruit the power of the system to help us navigate our days differently and write new stories of safety and connection." —*Polyvagal Practices*, p. 69

120 "When we learn to mindfully meet our nervous system, bring compassion to our embodied experiences, and honor our autonomic response, we have begun to befriend our nervous system." —*Polyvagal Exercises for Safety in Connection*, p. 42

122 "As our ventral, sympathetic, and dorsal energies ebb and flow, how we experience the world changes." —*Polyvagal Exercises for Safety in Connection*, p. 103

124 "While we are serious beings, problem-solvers wanting to make sense of the

world, we are also playful beings wanting to let go of our problems for a moment in time." —*Polyvagal Exercises for Safety in Connection*, p. 88

126 "Imagine you're an autonomic explorer learning about your nervous system." —*Anchored*, p. 37

128 "When we are firmly anchored in the ventral state, we feel truly embodied, present, safe, and ready to engage. Our brain adds information to help us engage with the world in an organized and resourceful way." —*Polyvagal Practices*, p. 129

130 "Resilience helps us stay hopeful when things feel hopeless, engage an effective survival response in the face of danger, manage levels of stress in an ongoing stressful environment, and keep moving forward when the world around us is filled with suffering." —*Polyvagal Exercises for Safety in Connection*, p. 159

132 "In any building design, the foundation is the most important element. It is the ground upon which the structure rests. For humans, safety is the foundation. When the autonomic nervous system senses safety, the footings are deep and secure. When the system senses danger, the ground feels shaky." —*Polyvagal Theory in Therapy*, p. 118

134 "Within a co-regulated relationship, our quest for safety is realized, and we find sanctuary in the co-created experience of connection." —*Polyvagal Practices*, p. 51

136 "The pathways to safety are wired into your biology and are waiting for you." —*Polyvagal Practices*, p. 16

138 "Reciprocity is the mutual ebb and flow that defines nourishing relationships." —*Polyvagal Theory in Therapy*, p. 26

140 "We depend on the vagal brake's capacity to relax and reengage as we navigate the demands of a normal day." —*Polyvagal Theory in Therapy*, p. 29

142 "The vagal brake releases and reengages, resourcing our ability for curiosity, communication, and cooperation." —*Polyvagal Theory in Therapy*, p. 108

144 "The process of looking at what stretches and what stresses our system is a way to create just the right degree of challenge to invite in new patterns and deepen ones that are already working." —*Polyvagal Practices*, p. 70

146 "Learning to listen to the wisdom of the autonomic nervous system and honoring the right degree of challenge is the foundation for change." —*Polyvagal Practices*, p. 70

148 "We are living a story that originates in our autonomic state, is sent through autonomic pathways from the body to the brain, and is then translated by the brain into the beliefs that guide our daily experience." —*Polyvagal Practices*, p. 43

150 " [I can] move out of the self-critical story of who I am into curiosity about how I respond." —*Polyvagal Theory in Therapy*, p. 67

152 "Humans are meaning-making beings, automatically pulled toward story." —*Polyvagal Exercises for Safety in Connection*, p. 156

154 "We make sense of the world by making comparisons. It is a normal part of our daily experience." —*Polyvagal Theory in Therapy*, p. 107

156 "As we learn that our nervous system works in accordance with the same survival systems all humans share, we begin to make space for self-compassion." —*Polyvagal Theory in Therapy*, p. 119

158 "We are all on an autonomic journey—an adventure that includes survival and safety, protection and connection." —*Polyvagal Practices*, p. 111

160 "The autonomic nervous system has an inherent longing to be in ventral . . . and an inherent knowing about how to get there." —Foundations of Polyvagal Practice Workshop

162 "Touch can activate our survival responses or help us anchor in safety." —*Polyvagal Practices*, p. 80

164 "Our brain and body are intimately connected, autonomic state and psychological story forming experiences and expectations that are sometimes nourishing and sometimes painful. Through the art of reflection we have the power to shape our systems in the direction of safety and connection." —*Polyvagal Exercises for Safety in Connection*, p. 140

166 "Awe brings a sense of wonder. It challenges our ordinary ways of thinking. For a moment, we step out of ourselves and our usual ways of being in the world." —*Polyvagal Theory in Therapy*, p. 187

168 "Awe is a state of wonder, curiosity, reverence, and deep appreciation. It exists along a continuum of ordinary to extraordinary, from everyday moments that are awe-inspiring to the profound moments when we are awestruck." —*Polyvagal Practices*, p. 97

BIBLIOGRAPHY

Dana, D. (2018). *Polyvagal theory in therapy: Engaging the rhythm of regulation.* Norton.

Dana, D. (2020). *Polyvagal exercises for safety and connection: 50 client-centered practices.* Norton.

Dana, D. (2021). *Anchored: How to befriend your nervous system using polyvagal theory.* Sounds True.

Dana, D. (2022). *Polyvagal card deck: 58 practices for calm and change.* Norton.

Dana, D. (2023). *Polyvagal practices: Anchoring the self in safety.* Norton.

ABOUT THE AUTHORS

Deb Dana, LCSW, is a clinician, consultant, and author who lectures internationally on how Polyvagal Theory informs work with trauma survivors. Deb's work shows how we can use the organizing principles of Polyvagal Theory to change the way we navigate our daily lives. She is well known for translating Polyvagal Theory into a language and application that are both understandable and accessible—for clinicians and curious people alike. She is the author of *Polyvagal Theory in Therapy, Polyvagal Exercises for Safety and Connection, Polyvagal Practices, The Polyvagal Flip Chart,* and *The Polyvagal Card Deck,* all available from Norton, and *Anchored,* available from Sounds True. You can learn more about Deb's work at rhythmofregulation.com.

Courtney Rolfe, LCPC, is a licensed therapist, speaker, and trainer passionate about bringing Polyvagal Theory to the world. Courtney believes that learning does not stop at cognitive understanding, and that it is the embodiment of the Polyvagal Theory principles that truly creates change. This is where Courtney's passion lies: in supporting and teaching clinicians, helping individuals and communities heal, and most importantly, in living the model. Courtney brings the wisdom of the nervous system into social justice and antiracism work, believing that understanding the nervous system is fundamental in creating safety and promoting equity. You can learn more about Courtney and her work at www.modernmindandheart.com.